Essential Mathematics
for GCSE Higher tier

Homework book

Michael White

Elmwood Press

First published 2006 by
Elmwood Press
80 Attimore Road
Welwyn Garden City
Herts AL8 6LP
Tel. 01707 333232

Reprinted 2012

ISBN 978 1 902 214 603

Typeset and illustrated by TnQ Books and Journals Pvt. Ltd., Chennai, India.

Printed and bound by Bookwell

Contents

NUMBER 1 1

TASK M1.1

Do not use a calculator.

1 Find the value of each calculation below:

    a $\dfrac{16 - 4}{2 + 4}$ **b** $\dfrac{3^2 + 4^2}{10 - 5}$ **c** $\dfrac{(11 + 4) \times (18 - 13)}{5^2}$

    d $\sqrt{(5^2 + 12^2)}$ **e** $\dfrac{4 \times 4 + 4}{4 \times 10}$ **f** $\dfrac{6 + 9 \div 3}{(19 + 17) \div 4}$

2 36 people pay a total of £936 to visit the theatre. If each person pays the same amount, how much does each person pay?

3 A box of crisps contains 48 packets. How many packets will there be in 263 boxes?

4 Write down the answer to each of the following:

    a $0{\cdot}4 \times 0{\cdot}6$ **b** $0{\cdot}07 \times 0{\cdot}5$ **c** $6 - 1{\cdot}03$ **d** $20 \times 0{\cdot}06$

    e $0{\cdot}3^2$ **f** $0{\cdot}81 \div 0{\cdot}3$ **g** $5{\cdot}7 \div 0{\cdot}03$ **h** $1{\cdot}8 \times 15$

    i $0{\cdot}36 \times 2{\cdot}7$ **j** $0{\cdot}02^3$ **k** $0{\cdot}6 \div 0{\cdot}003$ **l** $600 \times 0{\cdot}12$

5 How many 0·45 litre cartons of milk are needed to give 5·4 litres in total?

6 Croissants are loaded into trays of 32. How many trays are used to deal with 1400 croissants?

7 Which is larger? $3\sqrt{36}$ or $4\sqrt{25} - 2\sqrt{4}$

TASK M1.2

1 Work out and give the answer in its simplest form:

    a $\dfrac{5}{8} \times \dfrac{8}{9}$ **b** $\dfrac{7}{12} \times \dfrac{3}{14}$ **c** $\dfrac{3}{4} \times 20$ **d** $\dfrac{3}{5} \div \dfrac{9}{10}$

    e $\dfrac{4}{9} \div \dfrac{1}{3}$ **f** $2\dfrac{1}{2} \times \dfrac{7}{10}$ **g** $3\dfrac{1}{3} \times 1\dfrac{4}{5}$ **h** $6\dfrac{1}{4} \div 1\dfrac{3}{7}$

2 Gary gives $\dfrac{2}{3}$ of his money to Carol. Carol gives $\dfrac{6}{7}$ of this money to Zak. What fraction of Gary's money does Zak get?

3 Work out and give the answer in its simplest form:

    a $\dfrac{1}{4} + \dfrac{2}{3}$ **b** $\dfrac{5}{6} - \dfrac{3}{8}$ **c** $3\dfrac{3}{4} + 1\dfrac{5}{12}$ **d** $5\dfrac{1}{3} - \dfrac{7}{8}$

4 How many minutes longer does it take Denise to complete a job in three-quarters of an hour than Simon who completes the job in five-twelfths of an hour?

5 Annie and Chad walk from a pub in the same direction. If Annie has walked five-eighths of a mile and Chad has walked seven-tenths of a mile, how far apart are they?

6 Work out and give the answer in its simplest form:

a $\frac{1}{4} \times \frac{6}{7} + \frac{1}{2}$ **b** $\frac{8}{9} \div \frac{2}{3} - \frac{1}{6}$ **c** $\left(3\frac{2}{3} - 2\frac{3}{5}\right) \div \frac{2}{5}$

7 A piece of paper measures $8\frac{1}{4}$ cm by $7\frac{1}{3}$ cm. A square of side $2\frac{1}{2}$ cm is cut out and thrown away.
Show that the area that is left is exactly $54\frac{1}{4}$ cm^2.

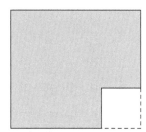

8 A photo measures $7\frac{1}{2}$ cm by $7\frac{1}{5}$ cm. Both its dimensions are increased by a factor of $1\frac{1}{3}$. Find the area of the enlarged photo.

TASK M1.3

Use a calculator.

1 Each of the calculations below is wrong. Find the correct answer for each calculation.

a $\frac{48 + 32}{20} = 49\cdot6$ **b** $\frac{51 - 31}{10} = 47\cdot9$ **c** $\frac{50}{25 \times 10} = 20$ **d** $\frac{75}{40 - 20} = -18\cdot125$

2 Work out the following, giving answers to the *nearest whole number*.
Match each calculation to the correct answer.

A $\left(\; 16 + 4\cdot9 - 3\cdot17 \;\right)$ P $\boxed{7}$

B $\left(\; 3\cdot4 \times (5\cdot8 - 4\cdot25) \;\right)$ Q $\boxed{4}$

C $\left(\; 8\cdot7 + \dfrac{2\cdot4}{1\cdot6} \;\right)$ R $\boxed{18}$

D $\left(\; \dfrac{35\cdot2}{(4\cdot9 - 0\cdot18)} \;\right)$ S $\boxed{10}$

E $\left(\; \dfrac{24\cdot63}{2\cdot17 + 3\cdot42} \;\right)$ T $\boxed{3}$

F $\left(\; \dfrac{13\cdot8 + 9\cdot16}{2\cdot4 \times 3\cdot7} \;\right)$ U $\boxed{5}$

3 A Bureau de Change offers $1·568 per £ but charges a commission fee at £3. How many dollars (to the nearest cent) do you get for £75?

4 Which is larger? $\left(3\frac{2}{5}\right)^2$ or $20\frac{1}{4} \div 1\frac{7}{9}$

A   B

5 Write the numbers below in order of size, starting with the smallest.

3^4 2^7 5^3 1^9 4^4

6 Calculate the following, giving each answer to 3 significant figures.

a $\dfrac{17·2 + 8·16}{8·61 - 2·48}$ **b** $3\sqrt{8} - 5$ **c** $\dfrac{(-9·1)^2 + 7·13}{(-4·28)^2}$

d $\dfrac{\sqrt{8} + \sqrt{2}}{\sqrt{7} - \sqrt{3}}$ **e** $\dfrac{-7·3 + (-1·9)^2}{(-1·72) \times (-2·4)}$ **f** $(\sqrt{6} - \sqrt{8})^4$

TASK M1.4

1 Convert the decimals below into fractions in their lowest form.
    a 0·7   **b** 0·35   **c** 0·035   **d** 0·92
    e 0·618   **f** 0·3185   **g** 0·713   **h** 0·625

2 By changing each fraction into a decimal, write the following fractions in order of size, starting with the smallest.

$\dfrac{3}{20}$ $\dfrac{1}{4}$ $\dfrac{3}{10}$ $\dfrac{5}{16}$ $\dfrac{3}{25}$ $\dfrac{45}{200}$

3 Use division to convert the fractions below into recurring decimals:

a $\dfrac{2}{9}$ **b** $\dfrac{5}{12}$ **c** $\dfrac{5}{6}$ **d** $\dfrac{5}{13}$ **e** $\dfrac{6}{7}$

4 Convert $\dfrac{137}{999}$ into a recurring decimal.

TASK E1.1

1 Copy and complete to change $0·\dot{7}\dot{4}$ to a fraction.

         let f = 0·74 74 74 ...

     100f = ⬚

we have f = 0·74 74 74 ...
subtract
      99f = ⬚

        f = $\dfrac{⬚}{⬚}$

2 Express the following recurring decimals as fractions in their lowest form:

a $0.\dot{7}$ b $0.\dot{2}\dot{8}$ c $0.646464...$

d $0.3\dot{8}\dot{2}$ e $0.57777....$ f $5.6\dot{8}\dot{4}$

3 Express $0.7\dot{1}\dot{5}$ in the form $\frac{a}{b}$ where a and b are integers (whole numbers).

TASK E1.2

1 $\sqrt{12} = \sqrt{4 \times 3} = \sqrt{4}\sqrt{3} = 2\sqrt{3}$ This is the simplified answer.
Simplify

a $\sqrt{18}$ b $\sqrt{32}$ c $\sqrt{72}$ d $\sqrt{20}$

e $\sqrt{125}$ f $\sqrt{28}$ g $\sqrt{300}$ h $\sqrt{54}$

2 Simplify as far as possible

a $\sqrt{7} \times \sqrt{5}$ b $\sqrt{2} \times \sqrt{5} \times \sqrt{3}$ c $(\sqrt{7})^2$

d $\sqrt{32} \div \sqrt{8}$ e $\frac{\sqrt{12}}{\sqrt{6}}$ f $\frac{\sqrt{30}}{\sqrt{5}}$

g $3\sqrt{2} \times 6\sqrt{3}$ h $2\sqrt{5} \times 4\sqrt{2}$ i $(2\sqrt{7})^2$

3 Which of the statements below are true?

a $\sqrt{14} \div \sqrt{2} = \sqrt{7}$ b $\sqrt{18} - \sqrt{8} = \sqrt{10}$ c $\sqrt{5} + \sqrt{9} = \sqrt{14}$

4 Simplify as far as possible

a $7\sqrt{3} - 5\sqrt{3}$ b $3\sqrt{5} + 3\sqrt{5}$ c $5\sqrt{2} - \sqrt{18}$

d $4\sqrt{2} + \sqrt{8}$ e $7\sqrt{6} - \sqrt{24}$ f $\sqrt{8} + \sqrt{50}$

g $\sqrt{80} - \sqrt{45}$ h $2\sqrt{5} \times 2\sqrt{5}$ i $5\sqrt{2} \times 3\sqrt{2} \times 4\sqrt{2}$

j $\sqrt{63} - \sqrt{28}$ k $\sqrt{75} + \sqrt{12} - \sqrt{108}$ l $(2\sqrt{3})^3$

TASK E1.3

1 Prove that $(\sqrt{3} + \sqrt{2})(\sqrt{3} - \sqrt{2}) = 1$.

2 Prove that $(\sqrt{5} + \sqrt{2})(\sqrt{5} + \sqrt{2}) = 7 + 2\sqrt{10}$.

3 Expand and simplify

a $(\sqrt{2} + 5)(\sqrt{3} + 2)$ b $(\sqrt{3} + \sqrt{7})(\sqrt{5} + \sqrt{2})$ c $(\sqrt{8} - \sqrt{5})(\sqrt{2} + \sqrt{3})$

d $(\sqrt{6} - 1)(\sqrt{6} + 1)$ e $(\sqrt{3} + 4)^2$ f $(\sqrt{7} - \sqrt{5})^2$

4 Find the 'exact' value of

a the area of this rectangle

b the perimeter of this rectangle

$(5 + \sqrt{3})\,\text{cm}$

$(2 - \sqrt{3})\,\text{cm}$

5 Rationalise the denominator in each of the following:

a $\dfrac{1}{\sqrt{6}}$ b $\dfrac{2}{\sqrt{3}}$ c $\dfrac{\sqrt{3}}{\sqrt{7}}$

d $4\dfrac{\sqrt{5}}{\sqrt{3}}$ e $\dfrac{\sqrt{5}-\sqrt{2}}{\sqrt{3}}$ f $\dfrac{\sqrt{3}+1}{\sqrt{5}}$

6 Simplify the following as far as possible:

a $\sqrt{8}\times\sqrt{6}$ b $\sqrt{15}\times\sqrt{5}$ c $\dfrac{21}{\sqrt{7}}$

d $3\sqrt{3}(\sqrt{2}-\sqrt{3})$ e $\sqrt{8}-\dfrac{2}{\sqrt{2}}$ f $(\sqrt{6}-2)^2$

g $\sqrt{12}+\dfrac{9}{\sqrt{3}}$ h $(\sqrt{5}-\sqrt{3})(\sqrt{3}+\sqrt{2})$ i $(\sqrt{7}-2)(\sqrt{7}+2)$

j $(\sqrt{3}+5)^3$ k $4\sqrt{3}(1+\sqrt{5})$ l $\dfrac{\sqrt{45}-3}{\sqrt{5}-1}$

NUMBER 2   2

TASK M2.1

Use a calculator when needed. Give answers to the nearest penny when needed.

1 a Decrease £70 by 3%   b Increase £68 by 2%
   c Decrease £264 by 46%   d Increase £89 by 12%

2 Carl's caravan is worth £15 500. One year later it is worth 6% less. How much is the caravan now worth?

3 A cinema increases its prices by 8%. If a ticket was £6·50, what would it cost after the increase?

4 A tin of baked beans costs 42p. Its price increases by 9% over the next 12 months. How much will the tin cost now? (remember to give your answer to the nearest penny)

5 A new car exhaust costs £88 + VAT. If VAT is 17·5%, work out the total cost of the car exhaust.

6 Write down the percentage multiplier that could be used for the following (eg. 'increase of 4%' means the percentage multiplier is 1·04).
  a increase of 15%   b decrease of 7%   c decrease of 42%
  d increase of 8·5%   e reduction of 24%   f increase of 17·5%

7 If VAT is 17·5%, find the price including VAT of each of the following:

a microwave £126   b carpet £870

c digital camera £220   d kettle £34

8 A shop reduces all its prices by 12%. If a necklace originally costs £84, how much will it now cost?

9 Jason buys a house for £185 000 but is forced to sell it quickly at a loss of 9%. How much does he sell the house for?

10 An eternity ring costs £680 + VAT (17·5%).
   a What is the total price of the ring?
   b In the Summer sales, the price of the ring is reduced by 20%. How much does the ring cost in the sales?

TASK M2.2

Use a calculator when needed. Give answers to one decimal place if necessary.

1 Ryan buys a mobile for £240 and sells it one year later for £204. What was his percentage loss?

2 Kelly buys a car for £300 and works on it before selling it for £420. What was the percentage profit?

3 A supermarket increases its workforce from 90 people to 117 people. What is the percentage increase?

4 Find the percentage increase or decrease for each of the following:

   a | original amount = 360 | final amount = 514·8 |

   b | original amount = 672 | final amount = 564·48 |

   c | original amount = 32 | final amount = 62·4 |

5 Leanne buys 100 books for £450. She sells each book for £5·40. Find the percentage profit Leanne makes on the books.

6 Sam buys 70 scarves at £5 each. He sells 40 of the scarves for £11 each but fails to sell the other scarves. Find the percentage profit he makes.

7 Joe buys a flat for £70 000 and sells it for £85 000.
Mo buys a house for £192 000 and sells it for £230 000.
Who makes the larger percentage profit and by how much?

8 The length, width and height of this cuboid are each increased by 15%.
What is the percentage increase in the volume of this cuboid?

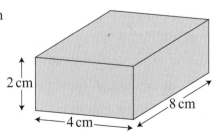

2 cm

8 cm

4 cm

9 Sandra's ideal body weight is 57 kg. During a period of six months her weight increases by 10%. During the next three months her weight returns to its ideal 57 kg. What was the percentage decrease from her heaviest weight back to her ideal weight?

TASK M2.3

Use a calculator when needed. Give answers to the nearest penny if necessary.

1 Tina invests £8000 in a bank at 5% per annum (year) compound interest. How much money will she have in the bank after 2 years?

2 A motorbike loses 25% of its value every year. Jennifer bought it for £720. How much would it be worth after:
a 2 years **b** 3 years

3 A bank pays 7% per annum compound interest. How much will the following people have in the bank after the number of years stated?
a Callum: £5000 after 2 years **b** Megan: £3500 after 2 years
c Lauren: £20 000 after 3 years **d** Oliver: £900 after 2 years

4 Which of the following will earn more money in 2 years?
A £4000 at 5·6% p.a. *simple* interest *or* **B** £4000 at 5·5% p.a. compound interest

5 A building society offers 8% p.a. compound interest. Candice puts £560 into the building society.
a Write down the *percentage multiplier* which could be used to find out how much money is in the building society after 1 year.
b How much money would be in the building society after 5 years?

6 A boat is worth £28 000. Its value depreciates (goes down) by 12% of its value each year. How much will the boat be worth after:
a 3 years **b** 10 years

7 The value of a house increases by 9% of its value each year. If a house is worth £170 000, how much will it be worth after:
a 2 years **b** 7 years **c** 20 years

8 Vikram invests some money in a bank at 12% p.a. compound interest. After how many years will his money have trebled?

8

TASK M2.4

Use a calculator when needed.

1 Ron's height has increased by 5% over the last year. He is now 1·89 m tall. How tall was he one year ago?

2 Katy now pays £129·60 rent each week after an 8% rent increase. How much did she pay before the increase?

3 Don buys a computer. A year later he sells it for £1200 at a loss of 20%. How much did Don pay for the computer?

4 'HARDTIMES' auto components have had to reduce their workforce by 12·5%. If 70 people now work for them, how many people worked for them before the job cuts?

5 Copy and complete the table below:

	Old price	% change	new price
a		9% increase	£33·79
b		40% decrease	£34·08
c		27% decrease	£70·08
d		8·5% increase	£56·42

6 A cricket bat costs £129·25 after VAT has been added on at 17·5%. How much did the cricket bat cost before VAT was added?

7 One week Arlene spends £75·60 on food which is 18% of her weekly pay. How much is her weekly pay?

8 A bike costs £399·50 including VAT at 17·5%. How much did the bike cost before VAT was added?

9 46 students from Year 10 in Grove Park School are ill one day. If this is 28·75% of all the Year 10 pupils, how many students are there in Year 10 in total?

10

DVD player £61 including VAT	In which shop is the DVD player cheaper and by how much? (VAT is 17·5%)	DVD player £52 + VAT
HOBB'S ELECTRICS		HEFTON'S

TASK M2.5

1 Change the following ratios to their simplest form.
    a 32 : 28   **b** 12 : 9 : 21   **c** 50 cm : 4 m   **d** 25p : £3

2 13 people pay £89·70 to visit a castle. How much would 28 people have to pay?

3 Cheese kebabs for 4 people need the ingredients below:

> 220 g   cheese
> 4   tomatoes
> 8   pineapple chunks
> $\frac{1}{2}$ cucumber

How much of each ingredient is needed for 10 people?

4 The recipe for making 20 biscuits is given below:

> 120 g   butter
> 50 g   caster sugar
> 175 g   flour

How much of each ingredient is needed for 24 biscuits?

4 Todd and Claire receive a total of 30 Christmas presents in the ratio 3 : 7. How many presents do each of them receive?

5 The angles p, q and r are in the ratio 7 : 2 : 3.
Find the sizes of angles p, q and r.

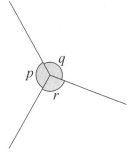

6 The ratio of boys to girls in a class is 6 : 5. How many girls are there in the class if there are 18 boys?

7 Paint is mixed by using yellow and blue in the ratio 7 : 2.
   a How much yellow is used if 8 litres of blue are used?
   b How much blue is used if 35 litres of yellow are used?
   c How much yellow and how much blue must be used to make 72 litres of the paint?

8 Des, Simone and Julie earn money in the ratio 3 : 2 : 5. If Des earns £27000 each year, how much do Simone and Julie each earn?

9 The ratio of weeds to flowers in a garden is 8 : 5. If there are 280 weeds in a garden, how many flowers are there?

TASK M2.6

1 Work out and write each answer as a number in index form:

   a $3^8 \div 3^3$

   b $2^3 \times 2^4 \times 2^2$

   c $5^3 \times 5 \times 5^3$

   d $5^6 \times 5^2 \div 5^4$

   e $(4^2)^3$

   f 8^0

   g $\dfrac{3^6 \times 3^4}{3^7}$

   h $6^2 \times (6^2)^2$

   i $\dfrac{7^4 \times (7^3)^2}{7^5}$

> **Remember:**
> $a^m \times a^n = a^{m+n}$
> $(a^m)^n = a^{mn}$
> $a^m \div a^n = a^{m-n}$
> $a^0 = 1$

2 Copy and complete:

a $3^4 \times \square = 3^9$ b $\square \times 6^3 = 6^7$ c $5^7 \div \square = 5^2$

d $8^{12} \div \square = 8^{11}$ e $\square \div 4^6 = 4^2$ f $(7^2)^3 \div \square = 7^2$

3 Simplify the expressions below:

a $x^4 \times x^3$ b $(x^2)^4$ c $a^6 \div a^2$

d $(a^0)^3$ e $(x^3)^2 \div x^2$ f $x^5 \div x$

4 Answer true or false for each statement below:

a $(x^4)^5 = x^9$ b $y^4 \times y^2 = y^8$ c $x^3 \times x = x^3$

d $\dfrac{n^6}{n} = n^5$ e $\dfrac{(x^3)^3}{(x^2)^3} = x^3$ f $\dfrac{(a^2)^4}{a} = a^6$

5 Simplify the expressions below:

a $\dfrac{(x^2)^6 \times x^2}{(x^7)^2}$ b $\dfrac{m^9}{m^2 \times m^5}$ c $\dfrac{n^{10}}{(n^3)^2 \times n^2}$

d $\dfrac{(x^3)^4 \times (x^2)^5}{(x^3)^6}$ e $\dfrac{m^{19}}{(m^2)^4 \times (m^5)^2}$ f $\dfrac{(x^3)^3 \times (x^2)^5}{(x^6)^2 \times (x^2)^2}$

6 Answer true or false for each statement below:

a $3x \times 3x = 9x^2$ b $5x^2 \times 4x^3 = 20x^6$

c $(3a^2)^2 = 9a^4$ d $\dfrac{15x^7}{3x^4} = 5x^3$

7 Simplify the expressions below:

a $3a^2 \times 2a^5$ b $(4b^2)^2$ c $\dfrac{40x^{10}}{5x^4}$

d $63m^7 \div 7m^5$ e $-9y^3 \times 4y^2$ f $(4n^3)^2$

TASK E2.1

1 3^{-2} (index form) $= \dfrac{1}{3^2} = \dfrac{1}{9}$ (ordinary number)

Write the following as ordinary numbers:

a 4^{-1} b 2^{-3} c 6^{-2} d 4^{-3}

e 10^{-2} f 5^{-3} g 7^{-1} h 2^{-6}

> Remember:
> $a^{-n} = \dfrac{1}{a^n}$

2 Write the following in negative index form:

a $\dfrac{1}{4^2}$ b $\dfrac{1}{3^4}$ c $\dfrac{1}{2^5}$ d $\dfrac{1}{8^3}$

3 Write $\dfrac{1}{25}$ as a power of 5 in negative index form.

4 Write $\dfrac{1}{27}$ as a power of 3 in negative index form.

5 Answer true or false for each statement below:

a $2^{-8} = \dfrac{1}{2^8}$ b $6^{-2} \times 6^{-2} = 6^{-4}$ c $9^{-1} = -9$

d $3^{-5} = \dfrac{5}{3}$ e $\left(\dfrac{1}{4}\right)^{-1} = 4$ f $\left(\dfrac{2}{3}\right)^{-2} = \dfrac{9}{4}$

6 Simplify the expressions below:

a $\dfrac{x^3 \times x^{-1}}{x^{-4}}$ b $(5x^{-3})^2$ c $\dfrac{4m^2 \times 3m^{-5}}{6m^{-2}}$

7 Write the following as ordinary numbers:

a $\left(\dfrac{1}{3}\right)^{-1}$ b $\left(\dfrac{3}{7}\right)^{-1}$ c $\left(\dfrac{3}{5}\right)^{-2}$ d $\left(\dfrac{2}{7}\right)^{-2}$

TASK E2.2

Do not use a calculator.

1 Evaluate the following:

a $25^{\frac{1}{2}}$ b $64^{\frac{1}{3}}$ c $1^{\frac{1}{3}}$

d $4^{-\frac{1}{2}}$ e $8^{-\frac{1}{3}}$ f $16^{\frac{1}{4}}$

g $100^{-\frac{1}{2}}$ h $216^{\frac{1}{3}}$

> **Remember:**
> $a^{\frac{1}{n}} = \sqrt[n]{a}$

2 Express the following as powers of 16:

a 4 b 1

c $\dfrac{1}{2}$ d $\dfrac{1}{16}$

3 Simplify the following:

a $\sqrt{x^6}$ b $(x^6)^{\frac{1}{2}}$ c $(x^6)^{\frac{1}{3}}$

d $\sqrt{25x^4}$ e $\sqrt[3]{8n^6}$ f $(27m^{12})^{\frac{1}{3}}$

g $(9a^6)^{-\frac{1}{2}}$ h $(64m^9)^{-\frac{1}{3}}$ i $(49a^2b^6)^{\frac{1}{2}}$

4 Evaluate the following:

a $121^{-\frac{1}{2}}$ b $\left(\dfrac{16}{25}\right)^{\frac{1}{2}}$ c $\left(\dfrac{81}{64}\right)^{-\frac{1}{2}}$

d $\left(\dfrac{9}{4}\right)^{-\frac{1}{2}}$ e $\left(\dfrac{8}{125}\right)^{\frac{1}{3}}$ f $\left(\dfrac{27}{64}\right)^{-\frac{1}{3}}$

g $\left(\dfrac{1}{216}\right)^{-\frac{1}{3}}$ h $\left(\dfrac{81}{10\,000}\right)^{-\frac{1}{4}}$

TASK E2.3

Do not use a calculator.

1 Copy and complete the following:

a $16^{\frac{3}{2}}$

$= (16^{\frac{1}{2}})^3$

$= (\square)^3$

$= \square$

b $8^{-\frac{2}{3}}$

$= \dfrac{1}{8^{\frac{2}{3}}}$

$= \dfrac{1}{\left(\square^{\frac{1}{3}}\right)^2}$

$= \dfrac{1}{\square^2}$

$= \dfrac{1}{\square}$

c $\left(\dfrac{25}{49}\right)^{-\frac{3}{2}}$

$= \left(\dfrac{\square}{\square}\right)^{\frac{3}{2}}$

$= \left(\dfrac{\square^{\frac{1}{2}}}{\square^{\frac{1}{2}}}\right)^{\square}$

$= \left(\dfrac{\square}{\square}\right)^{\square}$

$= \dfrac{\square}{\square}$

Remember:

$a^{\frac{m}{n}} = \sqrt[n]{a^m}$ or

$a^{\frac{m}{n}} = (\sqrt[n]{a})^m$

2 Evaluate the following:

a $36^{\frac{3}{2}}$ **b** $25^{\frac{3}{2}}$ **c** $16^{-\frac{3}{4}}$ **d** $125^{\frac{2}{3}}$

e $1000^{-\frac{2}{3}}$ **f** $81^{\frac{3}{4}}$ **g** $4^{-\frac{3}{2}}$ **h** $64^{-\frac{2}{3}}$

3 Simplify the following:

a $(4x^4)^{\frac{3}{2}}$ **b** $(27m^9)^{\frac{2}{3}}$ **c** $\sqrt{x} \times x\sqrt{x}$

d $\left(\dfrac{x^3}{8y^6}\right)^{-\frac{2}{3}}$ **e** $(16a^8b^4)^{\frac{3}{4}}$ **f** $(64m^{12}n^9)^{\frac{2}{3}}$

4 Evaluate the following:

a $\left(\dfrac{8}{27}\right)^{-\frac{2}{3}}$ **b** $\left(\dfrac{81}{16}\right)^{-\frac{3}{4}}$ **c** $\left(\dfrac{25}{4}\right)^{-\frac{3}{2}}$ **d** $\left(\dfrac{125}{64}\right)^{-\frac{2}{3}}$

5 Which of the statements below are true?

a $8^{-\frac{2}{3}} = \dfrac{1}{4}$ **b** $\left(\dfrac{16}{49}\right)^{-\frac{1}{2}} = \dfrac{-4}{7}$ **c** $\left(\dfrac{8}{125}\right)^{-\frac{2}{3}} = \dfrac{25}{4}$

TASK E2.4

1 Solve

a $3^x = 81$ **b** $7^x = 1$ **c** $8^x = \dfrac{1}{64}$

d $2^x = \dfrac{1}{4}$ **e** $2^x = \dfrac{1}{128}$ **f** $10^x = 0{\cdot}0001$

g $5^x = 0{\cdot}2$ **h** $5^x = \dfrac{1}{125}$ **i** $2^x = 0{\cdot}125$

2 Copy and complete:

a $16^x = 2$

$$\left(2^{\square}\right)^x = 2$$

$$2^{\square} = 2^1$$

$$\square = 1$$

$$x = \square$$

b $\left(\dfrac{1}{3}\right)^{\frac{x}{3}} = 27$

$$\left(3^{\square}\right)^{\frac{x}{3}} = 3^{\square}$$

$$\dfrac{-x}{3} = \square$$

$$x = \square$$

3 Solve

a $16^x = 4$

b $125^x = 25$

c $16^x = 32$

d $13^x = \dfrac{1}{169}$

e $49^x = \dfrac{1}{7}$

f $27^x = \dfrac{1}{9}$

g $8^x = \dfrac{1}{16}$

h $7^x = 49 \times \sqrt{7}$

i $2^x = \dfrac{4}{\sqrt{2}}$

4 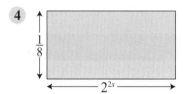 The areas of each rectangle are equal (all lengths are in cm). Find the value of x.

5 Solve

a $8^{4x} = \dfrac{1}{16}$

b $9^{x-2} = \dfrac{1}{27^x}$

c $125^{\frac{x}{2}} = \dfrac{1}{25^{x+1}}$

d $\left(\dfrac{1}{3}\right)^{2x} = \dfrac{1}{27}$

e $16^x = \dfrac{1}{(\sqrt{2})^4}$

TASK E2.5

1 Answer true or false for each statement below.

a $5n^{-1} = \dfrac{5}{n}$

b $(x^3)^2 = x^5$

c $\sqrt{(16a^4)} = 4a^4$

d $7^{-2} = \dfrac{2}{7}$

e $\left(\dfrac{4}{9}\right)^{-\frac{1}{2}} = \dfrac{3}{2}$

f $\dfrac{(x^4)^2 \times x^3}{x^7 \times x^4} = 1$

2 *Evaluate* without using a calculator:

a 3^{-2}

b $64^{-\frac{1}{3}}$

c $\left(\dfrac{1}{5}\right)^0$

d $\left(\dfrac{2}{7}\right)^{-1}$

e $16^{\frac{3}{2}}$

f $\left(\dfrac{4}{9}\right)^{\frac{1}{2}}$

g $\left(\dfrac{27}{125}\right)^{\frac{2}{3}}$

h $\left(\dfrac{49}{121}\right)^{-\frac{1}{2}}$

3 Simplify

a $(5a^2)^3$

b $\sqrt{(9m^6n^4)}$

c $(64x^{15})^{\frac{1}{3}}$

4 The area of this rectangle is 27 cm^2 (all lengths are in cm). Find the value of x.

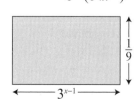

5 Simplify

   a $\dfrac{(4a^3b^4) \times (10a^2b^5)}{5a^4b^2}$ **b** $\dfrac{(6mn^2) \times (10m^3n^4)}{4mn^2}$

6 Express $\dfrac{128 \times 32^4}{64^3}$ as a power of 2.

7 Solve

   a $8^x = 2$ **b** $8^x = 4$ **c** $25^x = \dfrac{1}{5}$

   d $64^x = \dfrac{1}{16}$ **e** $4^{x+1} = \dfrac{1}{8^{2x}}$ **f** $27^{2x} = 81^{x-1}$

8 Find x if $\dfrac{4^x \times 16^2}{32^5} = 8$

SHAPE 1   3

TASK M3.1

Find the angles marked with letters.

1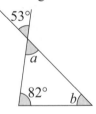

2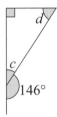

3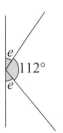

4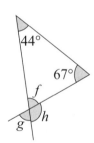

5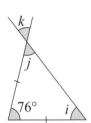

6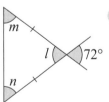

7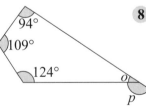

8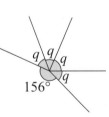

9 **a** Write down the value of $\angle ADB$.
     b Give a reason for your answer.
     c Find the value of $\angle CBD$.
     d Give full reasons for your answer.

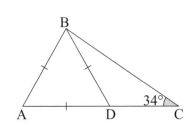

10 **a** Find the value of ∠QPR.
   b Give full reasons for your answer.

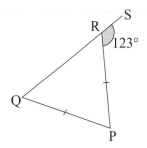

TASK M3.2

Find the angles marked with letters.

1

107°

a

2

b

39°

3

47°

c

d

4

110°

e *f*

g

5

124°

h *k*

i *j*

143°

6

l

86°

m *n*

o

54°

7

s

p

115° *r*

q

8

30°

u *t*

86°

v

9 **a** Find the value of ∠ABE.
   b Give full reasons for your answer.

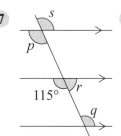

C

B

45°

A E 73° D

10 **a** Find the value of ∠SQR.
   b Give full reasons for your answer.

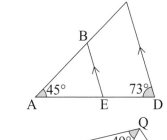

Q 49°

P

68° R

T S

TASK M3.3

1 Copy and complete below.
A pentagon can be split into _ _ _ _ triangles.
Sum of interior angles = _ _ _ _ × 180°
= _ _ _ _ °

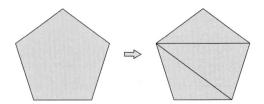

2 Find the sum of the interior angles of an octagon.

3 Find the sum of the interior angles of a polygon with 15 sides.

4 Copy and complete below.
This polygon can be split into _ _ _ _ triangles.
Sum of interior angles = _ _ _ _ × 180° = _ _ _ _ °
Add up all the given angles:
126° + 143° + 109° + 94° + 165° = _ _ _ _ °
angle x = _ _ _ _ °

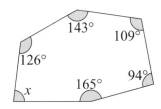

In the questions below, find the angles marked with letters.

5

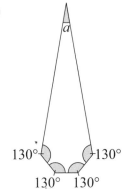

6

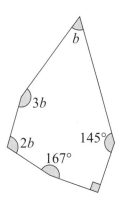

7

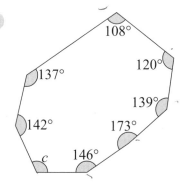

8 Nine of the ten interior angles of a decagon each equal 145°. Find the size of the other interior angle.

TASK M3.4

1 An octagon has 8 sides. Find the size of each exterior angle of a *regular* octagon.

2 A decagon has 10 sides.
   a Find the size of each exterior angle of a *regular* decagon.
   b Find the size of each interior angle of a *regular* decagon.

3 Find the size of angle *a*.

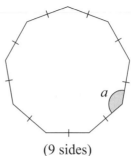

(9 sides)

4 Find the exterior angles of *regular* polygons with
    a 18 sides   **b** 24 sides   **c** 45 sides

5 Find the interior angle of each polygon in Question **4**.

6 The exterior angle of a *regular* polygon is 24°.
How many sides has the polygon?

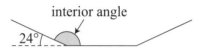

7 The interior angle of a *regular* polygon is 162°. How many sides has the polygon?

8 In a *regular* polygon, each exterior angle is 140° less than each interior angle. How many sides has the polygon?

9 Part of a *regular* dodecagon (12 sides) is shown. O is the centre of the polygon. Find the value of *x*.

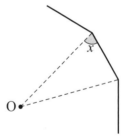

TASK M3.5

1 Prove that triangle QUT is isosceles.
Give all your reasons clearly.

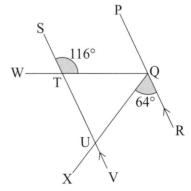

2 Prove that the sum of the angles in a quadrilateral add up to 360°.
Give all your reasons clearly.

In questions ③ to ⑧ , find the angle marked with letters.

③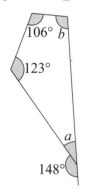

④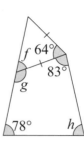

⑤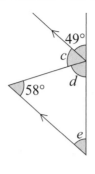

⑥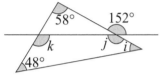

⑦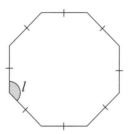

⑧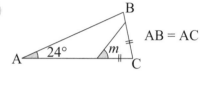

AB = AC

⑨ ABCD is a rectangle. Prove that triangle ABM is isosceles.
Give all your reasons clearly.

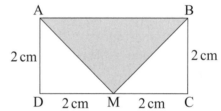

⑩ Prove that ∠ADC = ∠BAC.
Give all your reasons clearly.

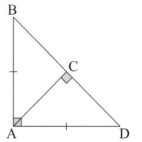

TASK E3.1

Find the angles marked with letters. (O is the centre of each circle)

①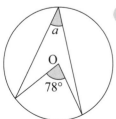

②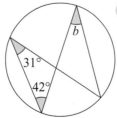

③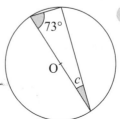

④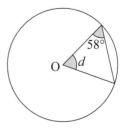

5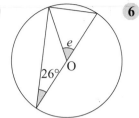

6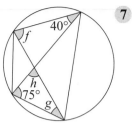

7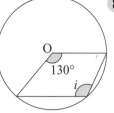

8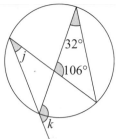

9 In this question, write down *all the reasons* for your answers.
Find
a ∠OEG
b ∠OGF
c ∠OFG
d ∠FEO
e ∠EFG

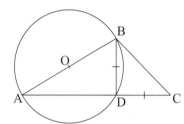

10 Find ∠BCD.
Write down *the reasons* for your answer.

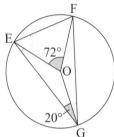

11 Find *x*

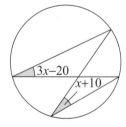

12 Find *y*

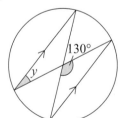

TASK E3.2

Find the angles marked with letters. (O is the centre of each circle)

1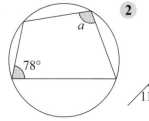

2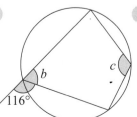

3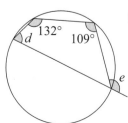

4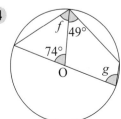

5 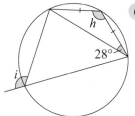 **6** 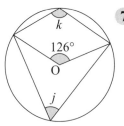 **7** 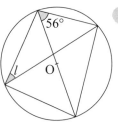 **8**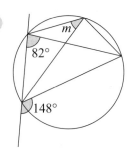

9 In this question, write down *all the reasons* for your answers.
Find
a ∠QRS
b ∠QOS
c ∠SQO

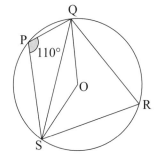

10 In this question, write down *all the reasons* for your answers.
Find
a ∠CDO
b ∠COD
c ∠ABC
d ∠AOC
e ∠AOD

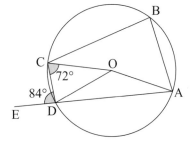

11 Find x

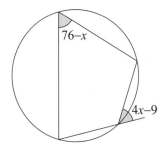

12 Find y

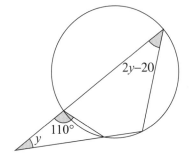

TASK E3.3

Find the angles marked with letters. (O is the centre of each circle)

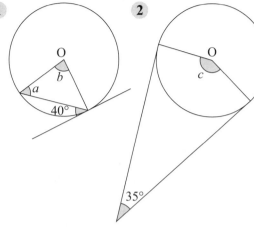

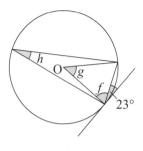

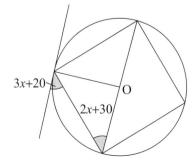

5 In this question, write down *all the reasons* for your answers.
Find
   a ∠BOC
   b ∠BDC
   c ∠CAB

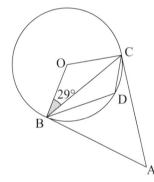

6 In this question, write down *all the reasons* for your answers.
Find
   a ∠POR
   b ∠PQO

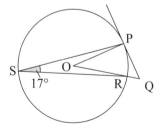

7 Find *x*

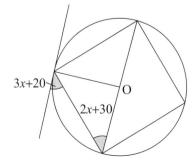

8 In each part of the question below, find *x* giving each answer to one decimal place.

a

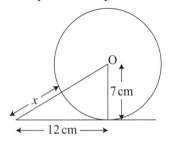

b

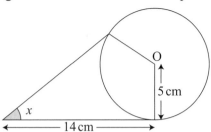

TASK E3.4

Find the angles marked with letters. (O is the centre of each circle)

1

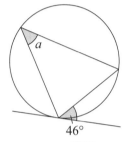

2

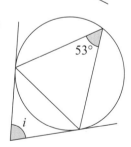

3

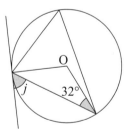

4

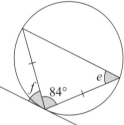

5

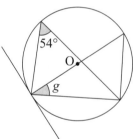

6

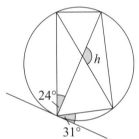

7

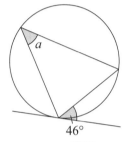

8

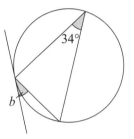

9 In this question, write down *all the reasons* for your answers.
Find
a ∠PQS
b ∠SUQ
c ∠SOQ

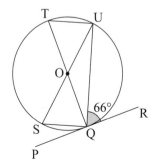

10 In this question, write down *all the reasons* for your answers.
Find
a ∠BDG
b ∠ABG
c ∠DBF

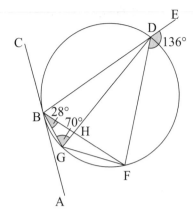

11 Find x

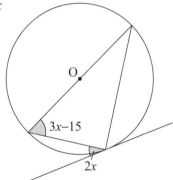

12 Find x and y

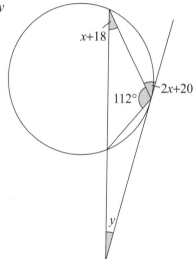

TASK E3.5

1 Prove that ∠PST = x (ie. the exterior angle of a cyclic quadrilateral equals the opposite interior angle).

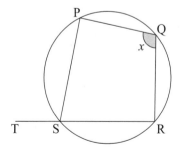

2 O is the centre of the circle. Copy and complete the statements below to prove that 'the angle at the centre of a circle is twice the angle at the circumference.'

∠OPQ = ☐ (triangle OPQ is isosceles)
∠POQ = ☐ (sum of angles in a triangle = 180°)

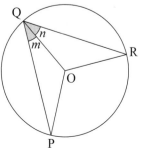

∠ORQ = ☐ (triangle ORQ is isosceles)
∠ROQ = ☐ (sum of angles in a triangle = 180°)
∠POR = 360 − ∠POQ − ∠ROQ (sum of angles at a point add up to 360°)
∠POR = 360 − (☐) − (☐)

$$= 360 - ☐ + ☐ - ☐ + ☐$$
$$= ☐ + ☐$$
$$= 2(☐ + ☐)$$

This proves that ∠POR = 2 × ∠PQR, ie. the angle at the centre of the circle is twice the angle at the circumference.

3 O is the centre of the circle.
Find the following angles in terms of *x* and y, *giving all your reasons.*
  a ∠DBE
  b ∠DFE
  c ∠GFD
  d ∠DOE
  e ∠OED

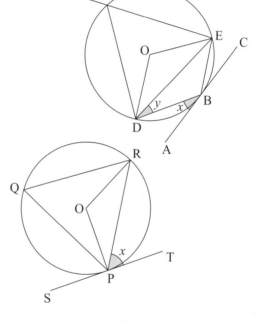

4 Prove the alternate segment theorem.

ALGEBRA 1   4

TASK M4.1

In Questions **1** to **20** find the value of each expression
when $f = -1$
       $g = 5$
       $h = -4$

1 $2h$ **2** $3f$ **3** fg **4** fh **5** $2g - h$

6 $3f + 4g$ **7** $4f + 3g$ **8** h^2 **9** $g^2 + h^2$ **10** $16 - h$

11 $f + g + h$ **12** $5g + 6f$ **13** $6h + 10$ **14** $3(f + g)$ **15** $7(g - f)$

16 $(4f)^2$ **17** $4g - 3f + 3h$ **18** $\dfrac{6h}{2f}$ **19** $\dfrac{7(f + g)}{h}$ **20** $2h^2$

In Questions **21** to **40** find the value of each expression
when $a = -2$
       $b = -5$
       $c = 3$

21 $a^2(c - b)$ **22** $3a^2$ **23** $(2b)^2 - 3b^2$ **24** $(4c)^2 + (5a)^2$

25 b^3 **26** $a(bc - a^2)$ **27** $\dfrac{2b + 4a}{3c}$ **28** a^2b^2

29 $b^2 + 6ab$ **30** $\dfrac{4c - 9a}{2b}$ **31** $a^2 + ac - b$ **32** $\dfrac{4b}{a} - \dfrac{10c}{b}$

33 $\dfrac{b(c^2 - a)}{a - c}$ **34** $a^3 + c^3$ **35** $(a - 2b)(2c - b)$ **36** $2c^3 - 2b^2$

37 $(a^2 - b)(a^2 + b)$ **38** abc **39** $4a^2bc$ **40** $\dfrac{b^2 + 5a^2}{c^2}$

TASK M4.2

1 The total surface area A of this cuboid is given
   by the formula
   $A = 2lw + 2lh + 2hw$
   Find the value of A when
   a $l = 5$, $w = 3$ and $h = 1$
   b $l = 10$, $w = 2\cdot5$ and $h = 4$

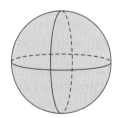

2 The total surface area A of a sphere is given
   by the formula
   $A = 12r^2$
   Find the value of A when
   a $r = 3$ **b** $r = 5$ **c** $r = 8$

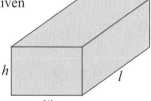

3 Energy E is given by the formula $E = mc^2$ where m is the mass and
   c is the speed of light.
   Find the value of E when $m = 15$ and $c = 300\,000\,000$.

4 The formula $s = ut + \dfrac{1}{2}at^2$ gives the displacement s of a particle after
   time t. The acceleration is a and the initial velocity is u.
   Find s (to 3 significant figures if necessary) when
   a $u = 3$, $t = 12$ and $a = 6\cdot4$ **b** $u = -8\cdot17$, $a = -9\cdot81$, $t = 4\cdot5$

5 The area A of a trapezium is given by the formula
   $A = \dfrac{1}{2}h(a + b)$
   Find the value of A when
   a $a = 6$, $b = 13$, $h = 12$ **b** $h = 3\cdot26$, $a = 4\cdot9$, $b = 7\cdot48$

6 The length of the diagonal AB is given by the
formula
$AB = \sqrt{(x^2 + y^2 + z^2)}$
Find the value of AB when $x = 13$ cm, $y = 8$ cm
and $z = 5$ cm. (give your answer to one
decimal place)

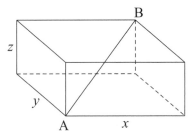

7 The mass m of a radioactive substance present at time t is given by the
formula
$m = 100(2^{-t})$
Find the value of m when
a $t = 0$ **b** $t = 1$ **c** $t = 4$

8 If $\frac{1}{f} = \frac{1}{u} + \frac{1}{v}$, find the value of f when $u = 8$ and $v = 17$.

TASK M4.3

In Questions **1** to **6** answer true or false.
1 $a + a = a^2$ **2** $5m + m = 6m$ **3** $6n^2 - n^2 = 6$

4 $4y \times y = 4y^2$ **5** $a \times 5 \times b = 5ab$ **6** $16x \div 4 = 12x$

Simplify
7 $4a \times -6b$ **8** $-3m \times -2p$ **9** $-15x \div 5$

10 $-3p \times 7q$ **11** $-a \times 3a$ **12** $-42a^2 \div -2$

Multiply out
13 $2(3y + 5)$ **14** $6(2a - b)$ **15** $7(2x + 5)$

16 $x(x - y)$ **17** $m(m - 3p)$ **18** $c(2d + 1)$

Write down and *simplify* an expression for the area of each shape below:

19
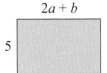
$2a + b$
5

20
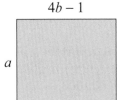
$4b - 1$
a

21
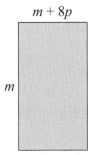
$m + 8p$
m

Expand
22 $-5(x - 3)$ **23** $-2(3m - 4)$ **24** $-m(2 - p)$

25 $-y(x + z)$ **26** $-x(x + 3y)$ **27** $-(a - b)$

28 $-q(q - 8r)$ **29** $3a(3a + 4b)$ **30** $-8x(4x - 3y)$

31 $-y(y^2 + 3x)$ **32** $4n^2(3n - 7)$ **33** $5xy(4x + 2y^2)$

34 $6ab(2a - 3b)$ **35** $8p^2q(3q - p)$ **36** $7m^2n^2(3n + 4mn^2)$

TASK M4.4

Expand and simplify

1 $3(a + 4) + 7$ 2 $9(2b + 4) + 4b$ 3 $7(5a + 6) - 10a$

Simplify

4 $3(8y + 6) + 2(2y - 5)$ 5 $5n + 9 + 6(2n + 3)$

6 $4b + 9(3b + 6) - 24$ 7 $7(4c + 7) + 3(2c - 8)$

Copy and complete

8 $6(3a + 2) - 4(2a + 2) = \square + 12 - \square - 8 = \square + 4$

9 $7(4x + 3) - 5(3x - 6) = 28x + \square - 15x + \square = 13x + \square$

Expand and simplify

10 $5(a + 4) - 3(a + 2)$ 11 $6(2m + 3) - 5(m + 3)$

12 $4(5y + 6) - 2(4y + 3)$ 13 $2(8b + 9) - 4(4b - 6)$

14 $8a - 3(2a - 5) + 6$ 15 $7x - 4(x - 1) - 3$

16 $9(4n + 7) - 5(2n + 4)$ 17 $10q + 3(5 - 2q) + 4(7q + 4)$

18 $3x(2x + 3) + 5x(x - 2)$ 19 $5n(3n - 4) - 2n(4n + 5)$

20 $4m(2m - n) - 3n(4m + n)$ 21 $3a(4a + 2b - 3c) - 4b(5a - 2c)$

TASK M4.5

Multiply out

1 $(x + 3)(x + 2)$ 2 $(m + 4)(m + 7)$ 3 $(c - 4)(c - 2)$

4 $(y - 8)(y + 2)$ 5 $(y - 7)(y + 3)$ 6 $(n - 9)(n - 4)$

7 Explain why $(x + 6)^2$ is *not* equal to $x^2 + 36$.

Expand

8 $(n + 7)^2$ 9 $(y - 4)^2$ 10 $(x - 8)^2$

Multiply out

11 $(3x + 2)(5x + 4)$ 12 $(5a + 4)(2a + 1)$ 13 $(2n - 4)(3n + 7)$

14 $(7y - 6)(3y - 2)$ 15 $(4a + 6)^2$ 16 $(5m - 9)^2$

17 $(6 + 5y)(6 + y)$ 18 $(9 - 4c)(7 + 2c)$ 19 $(4x - 2y)(8x + 3y)$

Expand and simplify

20 $(m + 4)^2 + (m + 7)^2$ 21 $(c + 6)^2 - (c - 1)^2$

22 Find the volume of this cuboid, simplifying your answer as far as possible.

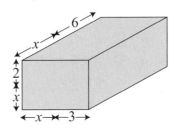

TASK M4.6

Copy and complete

1 $n^2 + 7n = n(n + \square)$

2 $4mp - 10m = 2m(2p - \square)$

3 $4ab + 18bc = 2b(\square + \square)$

4 $x^2y - 3xy^2 = xy(\square - \square)$

Factorise these expressions completely

5 $xy + yz$

6 $a^2 - 6a$

7 $b^2 + 4b$

8 $c^2 + 9c$

9 $mp - pq$

10 $3xy + 9xz$

11 $10ab - 15ac$

12 $18wz - 15wy$

13 $12fg + 21f$

14 $4a^2 - 6a$

15 $5p^2 - 30pq$

16 $18mp + 30m$

17 $8pq - 20q^2$

18 $16xyz - 28y^2$

19 $33a^2 + 55abc$

Factorise completely

20 $12m^2n - 9mn^2$

21 $25a^2b + 15abc$

22 $6x^2y + 15x^3$

23 $21m^3 - 28mn^2$

24 $48pq^2r - 36p^2qr$

25 $8xy^2 + 20xyz + 6yz^2$

26 $40a^3b - 56ab^2 + 32a^2b^3$

27 $36m^2n^3p^2 - 54mn^3p^3 - 27m^2n^2p^2$

TASK M4.7

Factorise the following

1 $x^2 + 12x + 35$

2 $m^2 + 12m + 27$

3 $y^2 - 4y + 3$

4 $n^2 - 2n - 24$

5 $a^2 - 6a - 27$

6 $c^2 - 8c - 20$

7 $n^2 - 11n + 24$

8 $y^2 - 14y + 45$

9 $a^2 + a - 30$

10 $x^2 - x - 72$

11 $p^2 + 15p + 44$

12 $m^2 + 4m - 60$

13 $a^2 - 15a + 56$

14 $q^2 + 4q - 96$

15 $b^2 - 5b - 150$

16 Write $x^2 + 2x + 1$ in the form $(x + a)^2$. Write down the value of a.

17 Write $x^2 + 8x + 16$ in the form $(x + b)^2$. Write down the value of b.

18 Write $x^2 - 6x + 9$ in the form $(x - c)^2$. Write down the value of c.

19 Write $x^2 - 14x + 49$ in the form $(x - d)^2$. Write down the value of d.

20 The total area of this shape is
$2x^2 - 10x + 29$
Find an expression for y in terms of x.

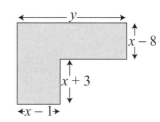

TASK E4.1

Factorise

1 $x^2 - y^2$ **2** $b^2 - 3^2$ **3** $y^2 - 5^2$ **4** $a^2 - 64$

5 $n^2 - 4$ **6** $p^2 - 1$ **7** $36 - x^2$ **8** $9y^2 - z^2$

9 $49 - 4a^2$ **10** $49x^2 - 81y^2$ **11** $144m^2 - 25$ **12** $16b^2 - \frac{1}{9}$

Copy and complete

13 $5x^2 - 20$
$= \square(x^2 - 4)$
$= \square(x + \square)(x - \square)$

14 $12a^2 - 27b^2$
$= 3(\square - \square)$
$= 3(\square + \square)(\square - \square)$

15 $4m^2 - 8m - 60$
$= 4(m^2 - \square - \square)$
$= 4(m + \square)(m - \square)$

Factorise completely

16 $3n^2 - 48$ **17** $50 - 2b^2$ **18** $5t^2 + 15t + 10$

19 $6n^2 - 42n + 60$ **20** $12p^2 - 147$ **21** $4x^2 - 16x - 48$

22 $7y^2 + 42y - 49$ **23** $80 - 45a^2$ **24** $32x^2 - 162y^2$

25 $9a^2 - 9a - 180$ **26** $10m^2 - 80m + 160$ **27** $72y^2 - 338$

TASK E4.2

Copy and complete

1 $mp + mq - np - nq$
$= m(\square + \square) - n(\square + \square)$
$= (\square + \square)(m - n)$

2 $a^2 - ac - ab + bc$
$= a(\square - \square) - b(\square - \square)$
$= (\square - \square)(a - b)$

Factorise

3 $mx + nx + my + ny$ **4** $ac - bc - ad + bd$

5 $pr + ps - qr - qs$ **6** $p^2 + pr - pq - qr$

7 $m^2 - mn - mk + kn$ **8** $ab - 3c + 3b - ac$

9 $8ac + 10ad + 4bc + 5bd$ **10** $20x^2 - 15xy + 16xz - 12yz$

TASK E4.3

Copy and complete

1 $5x^2 + 13x - 6$
$= 5x^2 + 15x - \boxed{} - 6$
$= 5x(\boxed{} + \boxed{}) - 2(\boxed{} + \boxed{})$
$= (\boxed{} + \boxed{})(5x - 2)$

2 $6x^2 - 19x + 10$
$= 6x^2 - 15x - \boxed{} + 10$
$= 3x(\boxed{} - \boxed{}) - \boxed{}(\boxed{} - \boxed{})$
$= (\boxed{} - \boxed{})(3x - \boxed{})$

Factorise each expression below

3 $5x^2 + 21x + 4$

4 $3a^2 + 20a + 12$

5 $10y^2 - 17y + 3$

6 $6n^2 - 13n - 5$

7 $14c^2 + 15c - 9$

8 $4x^2 - 81$

9 $20m^2 - 31m + 12$

10 $36a^2 + 19a - 6$

11 $200n^2 + 30n + 1$

12 $18p^2 - 25p - 3$

13 $100x^2 + 44x - 3$

14 $35m^2 - 69m + 28$

TASK E4.4

Copy and complete

1 $x^2 - 3x - 18 = 0$
$(x - 6)(x + \boxed{}) = 0$
$x - 6 = 0 \text{ or } x + \boxed{} = 0$
$x = \boxed{} \text{ or } x = \boxed{}$

2 $n^2 + 3n = 0$
$n(\boxed{} + \boxed{}) = 0$
$n = 0 \text{ or } \boxed{} + \boxed{} = 0$
$n = 0 \text{ or } n = \boxed{}$

3 $a^2 - 4a = 5$
$a^2 - 4a - \boxed{} = 0$
$(a + 1)(a - \boxed{}) = 0$
$a + 1 = 0 \text{ or } a - \boxed{} = 0$
$a = \boxed{} \text{ or } a = \boxed{}$

Solve these equations

4 $x^2 - 3x + 2 = 0$

5 $a^2 + 4a + 3 = 0$

6 $m^2 + 7m + 10 = 0$

7 $y^2 + y - 12 = 0$

8 $n^2 + 3n - 10 = 0$

9 $x^2 - 8x + 12 = 0$

10 $c^2 + 2c - 15 = 0$

11 $(m - 6)(m + 4) = 0$

12 $(a - 3)(a - 7) = 0$

13 $n^2 - 5n = 0$

14 $x^2 + 7x = 0$

15 $y^2 = 6y$

16 $p^2 + 5p = 14$

17 $n^2 + 32 = 12n$

18 $b^2 - 3b = 0$

19 $x^2 - 13x + 30 = 0$

20 $a^2 + 36 = 13a$

21 $m(m + 2) = 24 - 3m$

Solve the following equations

22 $3p^2 - 11p + 6 = 0$

23 $10a^2 - 3a - 1 = 0$

24 $8y^2 + 10y + 3 = 0$

25 $21m^2 - 41m + 10 = 0$

26 $4m^2 = m$

27 $4h^2 + 4h - 15 = 0$

28 $(9x - 1)(5x - 1) = 0$

29 $15w^2 - 14w = 8$

30 $4y^2 - 25 = 0$

31 $4h^2 - 12h + 8 = 0$

32 $5n^2 - 14 = 33n$

33 $n^3 - 3n^2 - 10n = 0$

TASK E4.5

1 The base of a triangle is 4 cm longer than its height. Let the height of the triangle be x.
   a If the area of the triangle is 30 cm^2, show that
   $x^2 + 4x - 60 = 0$
   b Find the base of the triangle.

2 A square piece of paper is trimmed to form a rectangle. One of its sides is reduced by 3 cm and the other side is reduced by 4 cm. The resulting rectangle has an area of 20 cm^2. If the side length of the initial square was s,
   a Write down a quadratic equation involving s
   b Solve this equation to find s

3 A square is adjoined by two rectangles, each of length 5 units. If the total area is then 39 square units, what is the length of the square?

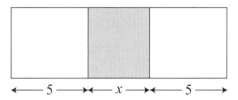

4 A rectangular garden measures 10 m by 15 m. Its width and length are then both increased by x metres. If its area is now 266 m^2, find x.

5 A small rectangular field is 5 m longer than it is wide. The diagonal of the field is 25 m.
   a If the width of the field is x, show that
      $x^2 + 5x - 300 = 0$
   b Find the dimensions of the field.

6 Two numbers differ by $\frac{1}{2}$. Their product is 68.
   a If the smaller number is x, show that
      $2x^2 + x - 136 = 0$
   b Write down the value of each number if they are positive.

7 A pencil box (in the shape of a cuboid) is 9 cm longer than it is wide and 1 cm higher than it is wide. The longest pencil which can be jammed into the case is 13 cm long. Find the dimensions of the pencil case.

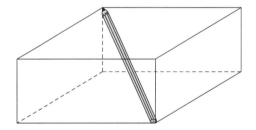

NUMBER 3   5

TASK M5.1

1 Which of these numbers are:
   a multiples of 6
   b multiples of 7
   c *not* multiples of 2

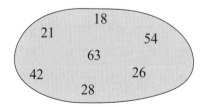

2 Write down all the factors of 35 which are prime.

3 Write down *all* the factors of 50.

4 **a** List all the factors of 18.
   b List all the factors of 30.
   c Write down the Highest Common Factor of 18 and 30.

5 Find the HCF of:
   a 25 and 60   **b** 36 and 90   **c** 16, 32 and 40

6 Add together all the prime numbers between 20 and 40.

7 Find the Lowest Common Multiple of:
   a 8 and 12   **b** 10 and 60   **c** 21 and 28

8 Amy and Josh are racing each other. Amy takes 5 minutes to complete one lap. Josh takes 7 minutes to complete one lap. After how many minutes will Amy and Josh pass the starting point at exactly the same time?

TASK M5.2

1 Work out
   a $3 \times 3 \times 5$ **b** $2^2 \times 7$ **c** $2^2 \times 3^2$

2 For each question below, find the number which belongs in the empty box:
   a $60 = 2^2 \times 3 \times \boxed{}$ **b** $40 = 2^3 \times \boxed{}$ **c** $126 = 2 \times 3^2 \times \boxed{}$

3 Using any method, write the following numbers as products of prime factors, leaving each answer in index form:
   a 75   **b** 44   **c** 80   **d** 594

4 $\boxed{1617 = 3 \times 7 \times 7 \times 11}$ and $\boxed{273 = 3 \times 7 \times 13}$

   Find the Highest Common Factor of 273 and 1617.

5 Write 315 and 495 as products of prime factors. Use this to find the Highest Common Factor of 315 and 495.

6 Use question **4** to find the Lowest Common Multiple of 273 and 1617.

7 Use question **5** to find the LCM of 315 and 495.

8 Find **a** the HCF and **b** the LCM of 396 and 420.

9 Find **a** the HCF and **b** the LCM of 198 and 220.

10 Gill saves £105 each week for x weeks. Matt saves £147 each week for y weeks. If Gill and Matt end up saving the same total amount of money, write down the smallest possible values for x and y.

TASK M5.3

1 Write the numbers below in standard form.

    a 3000   **b** 70 000   **c** 340   **d** 89 000

    e 486 000   **f** 598   **g** 9 million   **h** 76 million

> **Remember:**
> a standard form number will have the form $A \times 10^n$ where $1 \leqslant A < 10$

2 Remember that $570 = 5 \cdot 7 \times 10^2$ but $0 \cdot 057 = 5 \cdot 7 \times 10^{-2}$. Write the numbers below in standard form.

    a 0·004   **b** 0·0007   **c** 0·9   **d** 0·0018

    e 0·528   **f** 0·000019   **g** 0·0034   **h** 0·00000817

3 Write each number below as an ordinary number.

    a 6×10^4 **b** 3×10^2 **c** 3×10^{-2} **d** $5 \cdot 6 \times 10^4$

    e $2 \cdot 4 \times 10^5$ **f** $8 \cdot 6 \times 10^{-3}$ **g** $4 \cdot 16 \times 10^3$ **h** $7 \cdot 68 \times 10^{-1}$

4 $3700 = 37 \times 10^2$. *Explain* why this number is not written in standard form.

5 $28\,000 = 28 \times 10^3$. This number is not written in standard form.
   Write it correctly in standard form.

6 Write the numbers below in standard form.

    a 0·0007   **b** 53 000   **c** 0·096   **d** 0·487

    e 49 000 000   **f** 576 000   **g** 0·00 074   **h** 82·4

    i 0·1   **j** 0·000 000 864 **k** 6 180 000   **l** 42 000 000

TASK M5.4

Do not use a calculator.

1 Write each number below in standard form.

    a 73×10^4 **b** 42×10^{14} **c** $0 \cdot 8 \times 10^7$ **d** $0 \cdot 32 \times 10^{24}$

    e $0 \cdot 68 \times 10^{-4}$ **f** 374×10^{-7} **g** 425×10^{38} **h** $0 \cdot 56 \times 10^{-7}$

2 Find the area of this rectangle, leaving your answer in standard form.

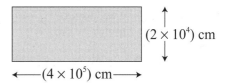

(2×10^4) cm

(4×10^5) cm

3 Work out the following, leaving each answer in standard form.

    a $(2 \times 10^8) \times (2 \cdot 5 \times 10^7)$ **b** $(1 \cdot 5 \times 10^6) \times (4 \times 10^3)$

    c $(3 \cdot 5 \times 10^9) \times (2 \times 10^{-4})$ **d** $(1 \cdot 7 \times 10^{-18}) \times (4 \times 10^{-8})$

    e $(4 \times 10^{12}) \times (3 \times 10^7)$ **f** $(9 \times 10^{17}) \times (4 \times 10^{28})$

    g $(8 \times 10^{21}) \div (4 \times 10^6)$ **h** $(7 \times 10^{19}) \div (2 \times 10^7)$

    i $\dfrac{9 \times 10^{32}}{4 \cdot 5 \times 10^{-5}}$ **j** $(4 \times 10^5)^2$

    k $(8 \cdot 7 \times 10^{12}) \div (3 \times 10^{-16})$ **l** $\dfrac{3 \times 10^{48}}{6 \times 10^{13}}$

4 Calli has £(4×10^5) and Carl has £(3×10^4). They put their money together. Write down the total amount of money they have, giving your answer in standard form.

5 Work out the following, leaving each answer in standard form.
 a $(5 \times 10^6) + (7 \times 10^5)$ **b** $(9 \times 10^8) - (4 \times 10^7)$ **c** $(4{\cdot}8 \times 10^{12}) - (1{\cdot}9 \times 10^{11})$
 d $(3 \times 10^{-2}) - (9 \times 10^{-3})$ **e** $(4{\cdot}3 \times 10^{-8}) + (2 \times 10^{-7})$ **f** $(6{\cdot}4 \times 10^{24}) + (5{\cdot}6 \times 10^{23})$

6 In a TV popstar show final, the number of votes for each contestant is shown below:

Gary Tallow ($9{\cdot}6 \times 10^5$) votes
Nina X ($1{\cdot}3 \times 10^6$) votes
Rosa Williams ($1{\cdot}85 \times 10^6$) votes

How many people voted in total?

7 Work out $(7 \times 10^{-12})^3$, leaving your answer in standard form.

8 The density of a type of stone is $3{\cdot}5 \times 10^4$ kg/m^3. Find the mass of this type of stone if its volume is 20 m^3, leaving your answer in standard form (mass = density × volume).

TASK M5.5

Use a calculator.

1 Work out the following and write each answer in standard form.
 a $(7 \times 10^8) \times (4 \times 10^9)$ **b** $(6{\cdot}2 \times 10^5) \times (3 \times 10^{34})$
 c $(4 \times 10^{-8}) \times (6 \times 10^{37})$ **d** $(3{\cdot}6 \times 10^{14}) \div (3 \times 10^{-14})$
 e $(7{\cdot}6 \times 10^{-29}) \div (2 \times 10^{-11})$ **f** $(5{\cdot}2 \times 10^{37}) + (6{\cdot}1 \times 10^{36})$

2 The population of the UK is ($5{\cdot}97 \times 10^7$) people. The population of the USA is ($2{\cdot}41 \times 10^8$) people. What is the combined population of the UK and USA? (give your answer in standard form)

3 The mass of an atom is $3{\cdot}74 \times 10^{-26}$ grams. What is the total mass of 2 million atoms?

4 Work out the following, leaving each answer in standard form correct to 3 significant figures.

 a $\dfrac{(5{\cdot}6 \times 10^{21}) \times (2{\cdot}7 \times 10^{28})}{5 \times 10^{13}}$ **b** $\dfrac{(7{\cdot}4 \times 10^{-13}) \times (3{\cdot}94 \times 10^{-26})}{4{\cdot}2 \times 10^{18}}$

 c $\dfrac{(3{\cdot}8 \times 10^{23}) - (9{\cdot}7 \times 10^{22})}{1{\cdot}8 \times 10^{-17}}$ **d** $\dfrac{(4{\cdot}89 \times 10^{16})^2}{2{\cdot}14 \times 10^9}$

 e $\dfrac{(4{\cdot}83 \times 10^{14}) + (3{\cdot}16 \times 10^{15})}{2{\cdot}82 \times 10^{-12}}$ **f** $\dfrac{5{\cdot}28 \times 10^{31}}{(4{\cdot}9 \times 10^{-10}) + (2{\cdot}7 \times 10^{-9})}$

 g $\dfrac{(7{\cdot}3 \times 10^{14})^2}{(3{\cdot}92 \times 10^{-15}) \times (2{\cdot}8 \times 10^{-23})}$ **h** $\dfrac{(3{\cdot}48 \times 10^{15}) \times (2{\cdot}19 \times 10^{26})}{(4{\cdot}37 \times 10^{12}) + (1{\cdot}95 \times 10^{11})}$

5 The adult population of a country is 60 million. The average annual income per adult is £27 000. Find in standard form the total annual income from the adult population.

6 In 2000 the population of a country was 9.2×10^9. Over the next five years the population rose by 15%. Find the population in 2005.

7 The diameter of the earth is 1.3×10^7 m. Assuming that the earth is a perfect sphere, find the circumference of the earth. Give your answer in standard form to 2 significant figures.

8 The population of a certain country is 5.7×10^8 and its area is 7.21×10^{10} m^2. Find the population density (people per m^2) of this country. Give your answer in standard form to 2 sig. figs.

9 The population of a certain type of bird increased from 7.8×10^3 to 1.2×10^4 over a ten year period. Find the percentage increase over that period, giving your answer to 3 sig. figs.

10 The speed of light is approximately 2.8×10^8 m/s. Express this in km/h in standard form to 3 sig. figs.

TASK M5.6

1 The length of a book is 23·4 cm, measured to the nearest 0·1 cm.

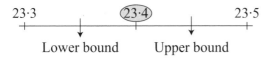

Write down **a** the lower bound **b** the upper bound

2 The width of a room is 3·8 m, measured to the nearest 0·1 m.
Write down **a** the lower bound **b** the upper bound

3 A woman weighs 63 kg, correct to the nearest kg. What is her least possible weight?

4 Copy and complete the table.

A length l is 47·2 cm, to the nearest 0·1 cm, so		$\leqslant l <$	47·25
A mass m is 83 kg, to the nearest kg, so		$\leqslant m <$	
A Volume V is 7·3 m^3, to the nearest 0·1 m^3, so		$\leqslant V <$	
A radius r is 6·87 cm, to the nearest 0·01 cm, so		$\leqslant r <$	
An area A is 470 m^2, to the nearest 10 m^2, so		$\leqslant A <$	

5 The base and height of a triangle are measured to the nearest 0·1 cm.

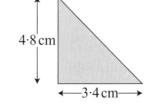

    a Write down the upper bound for the base 3·4 cm.

    b Write down the lower bound for the height 4·8 cm.

6 The capacity of a jug is 503·4 ml, measured to the nearest 0·1 ml. Write down

    a the lower bound   **b** the upper bound

7 In a 200 m race a runner is timed at 23·46 seconds to the nearest 0·01 second. Write down the greatest possible time.

8 A person weighs 64 kg, correct to the nearest 4 kg. The lower bound is 62 kg. Write down the upper bound.

9 The width of a lake is measured at 280 m, correct to the nearest 20 m. Write down the upper and lower bounds.

10 The mass of a substance is measured as 8·5 g, correct to the nearest 0·5 g. Write down the least possible mass of the substance.

TASK E5.1

1 The length, width and height of the cuboid are measured to the nearest cm.
volume = length × width × height
What is the lowest possible value of the volume of the cuboid?

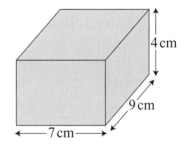

2 If $k = 1·8$, $m = 4·9$ and $n = 8·3$, all measured to one decimal place, calculate:

    a the smallest possible value of kn

    b the largest possible value (to 3 sig. figs) of $\frac{m}{k}$

    c the largest possible value of $m + n - k$

3 The base and height of this triangle are measured to the nearest 0·1 m.
Calculate the lower and upper bounds for the area of this triangle.

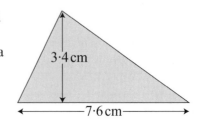

4 The acceleration a after time t can be calculated with
the formula
$$a = \frac{v - u}{t}$$
where v is the speed and u is the initial speed. If $v = 23$, $u = 18$ and
$t = 39$, measured to the nearest whole number, calculate:
a the minimum possible value for a (to 2 sig. figs)
b the maximum possible value for a (to 2 sig. figs)

5 The area of a square is given as 70 cm², correct to
the nearest cm².
Find the upper and lower bounds for the length x of
one side of the square.

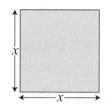

6 Pythagoras' theorem states that $a^2 + b^2 = c^2$ where a, b and c are the three lengths
of a right-angled triangle and c is the hypotenuse. If $a = 4\cdot3$ cm and $c = 12\cdot1$ cm,
both correct to 1 decimal place, find the upper and lower bounds for b.

TASK E5.2

1 m is directly proportional to n.
$m = 48$ when $n = 8$.
a Find the value of k such that $m = kn$.
b Find the value of m when $n = 5$.
c Find the value of n when $m = 72$.

> **Remember:**
> if $y \propto x$ then
> $y = kx$ where k is a
> constant

2 p is directly proportional to q.
$p = 28$ when $q = 4$.
a Find a formula for p in terms of q.
b Find p when $q = 9$.
c Find q when $p = 21$.

3 In the following tables, y is directly proportional to x. Copy and
complete each table.

a

x	6	11		22
y		54		108	

b

x	6	10		32
y		35	70	

4 In an electrical circuit it is known that the voltage V varies as the
current I (ie. that V is directly proportional to I). It is also known that
$V = 36$ when $I = 8$.
a Find a formula for V in terms of I.
b Find V when $I = 14$.
c Find I when $V = 27$.

5 A force F is directly proportional to its acceleration a.
$F = 31$ when $a = 5$.
a Find F when $a = 9$.
b Find a when $F = 80.6$.

TASK E5.3

1 Find k then copy and complete the table below given that $y = kx^3$.

x	3	5		10
y	135		1715	

2 Find k then copy and complete the table below given that $y = k\sqrt{x}$.

x	4	9		100
y	12		48	

3 m is directly proportional to the square root of n.
$m = 6$ when $n = 9$.
a Copy and complete:
$m \propto \sqrt{n}$ so $m = \boxed{}\sqrt{n}$
$m = 6, n = 9$ so $6 = \boxed{}\sqrt{\boxed{}}$
$6 = 3\boxed{}$
$\boxed{} = 2$
so $m = \boxed{}\sqrt{n}$
b Find m when $n = 25$.
Copy and complete:
$n = 25$ so $m = \boxed{}\sqrt{25} = \boxed{}$

4 L is directly proportional to the square of W.
$L = 24$ when $W = 2$.
a Find a formula for L in terms of W.
b Find L when $W = 5$.
c Find W when $L = 96$.

5 P is directly proportional to the cube of Q.
$P = 32$ when $Q = 4$.
a Find a formula for P in terms of Q.
b Find P when $Q = 6$.
c Find Q when $P = 500$.

6 **a** If y is directly proportional to x^2 then by what factor does y increase as x doubles?
b If y is directly proportional to x^3 then by what factor does y increase as x doubles?

7 The mass M of an object is directly proportional to the cube root of its height H.
$M = 20$ when $H = 64$.
a Find M when $H = 27$.
b Find H when $M = 35$.

TASK E5.4

1 Find k then copy and complete the table below given that $y = \frac{k}{x}$

x	1	4	8	
y		5		1

2 y is inversely proportional to x $\left(\text{ie. } y \propto \frac{1}{x} \text{ so } y = \frac{k}{x}\right)$.
$y = 16$ when $x = 2$.
a Write down an equation for y in terms of x.
b Find y when $x = 10$.
c Find x when $y = 4$.

3 R is inversely proportional to I.
When $I = 5$, $R = 3$.
a Write down an equation for R in terms of I.
b Find R when $I = 7\cdot5$.
c Find I when $R = 30$.

4 y is inversely proportional to the cube root of x.
$y = 30$ when $x = 8$.
a Write down an equation for y in terms of x.
Copy and complete:

$$y \propto \frac{1}{\sqrt[3]{x}} \qquad \text{so} \qquad y = \frac{k}{\sqrt[3]{x}}$$

$$y = 30, x = 8 \quad \text{so} \quad 30 = \frac{k}{\sqrt[3]{\square}}$$

$$30 = \frac{k}{\square}$$

$$k = \square$$

$$\text{so} \qquad y = \frac{\square}{\sqrt[3]{x}}$$

b Find y when $x = 1000$. Copy and complete:

$$x = 1000 \qquad \text{so} \qquad y = \frac{\square}{\sqrt[3]{\square}} = \frac{\square}{\square} = \square$$

c Find x when $y = 20$. Copy and complete:

$$y = 20 \qquad \text{so} \qquad 20 = \frac{\square}{\sqrt[3]{x}}$$

$$20\sqrt[3]{x} = \square$$

$$\sqrt[3]{x} = \frac{\square}{20} = \square$$

$$x = \square^3 = \square$$

5 m is inversely proportional to the square of v.
$m = 4$ when $v = 5$.
a Find an equation for m in terms of v.
b Find m when $v = 2$.
c Find v when $m = 0{\cdot}25$.

6 The width W of an object is inversely proportional to the cube of its height H.
$W = 2$ when $H = 2$.
a Find an equation for W in terms of H.
b Find W when $H = 4$.
c Find H when $W = \dfrac{1}{32}$.

7 x is inversely proportional to the square root of y.
$x = 3$ when $y = 100$.
a Find x when $y = 16$.
b Find y when $x = 12$.

ALGEBRA 2   6

TASK M6.1

Solve

1 $\dfrac{n}{4} = 2$ **2** $\dfrac{x}{10} = 6$ **3** $n + 3 = 1$ **4** $y + 2 = 1$

5 $p - 3 = -6$ **6** $3a = -6$ **7** $-5x = -20$ **8** $n \div 3 = -4$

9 $\dfrac{b}{5} = -5$ **10** $\dfrac{m}{7} = -3$ **11** $2y = 1$ **12** $7f = 2$

13 $2n = -3$ **14** $5x = 7$ **15** $7a = -4$ **16** $3m = -11$

17 Find the value of x in this rectangle.

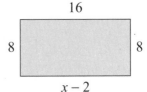

18 Pat thinks of a number and then adds 10. If the answer is 5, what number did Pat think of?

Solve the following equations

19 $6n + 4 = 16$ **20** $3a - 8 = 19$ **21** $34 = 5y - 6$

22 $4m + 7 = 10$ **23** $9w - 5 = 2$ **24** $8y - 2 = -5$

25 $5x - 3 = 2x + 18$ **26** $9p - 6 = 6p + 18$ **27** $5n + 3 = 27 - n$

28 $3a + 9 = 44 - 2a$ **29** $5w + 19 = 11 - 3w$ **30** $17 - 2x = 29 - 6x$

31 This is an *isosceles* triangle.
Find the value of x.

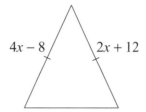

$4x - 8$ $2x + 12$

Solve

32 $\dfrac{8}{x} = 12$ **33** $\dfrac{n}{4} + 2 = 8$ **34** $\dfrac{m}{7} - 3 = 4$

35 $\dfrac{4a}{5} = 12$ **36** $\dfrac{6w}{5} = -12$ **37** $\dfrac{48}{c} = -4$

TASK M6.2

Solve

1 $2(2x + 3) = 14$ **2** $4(n - 3) = 24$ **3** $5(2a - 1) = 25$

4 $5(2w - 6) = 40$ **5** $5(2a + 3) = 18$ **6** $70 = 10(2 - 5y)$

7 I think of a number. I add 9 onto the number then multiply the answer by 3. This gives 36. What was the number I started with?

Solve the following equations

8 $4(2x + 1) = 2(3x + 5)$ **9** $5(3a + 4) = 4(3a + 20)$

10 $2(4y - 3) = 5(y + 6)$ **11** $4(3m - 1) = 2(5m + 7)$

12 $5(2n + 4) = 2(4n + 3)$ **13** $3(3w + 2) + 5(w + 4) = 54$

14 $8(3q + 4) + 1 = 3(12q - 1)$ **15** $5(2x + 1) - 5 = 2(6x + 5)$

16 $7 - 3(2 - 3x) = 10$ **17** $3(h - 2) + 2(h - 3) = 28$

18 $4(2p + 7) - 5(p - 1) = 12$ **19** $6(2a + 3) - 4 = 4(a + 6) + 6$

20 $3(2w + 7) - 5 = 4(3w - 6) + 35$ **21** $2(5x + 3) - 6(2x - 1) = 3(x + 14)$

TASK M6.3

Solve

1 $\dfrac{x}{7} - 4 = 4$ **2** $\dfrac{y - 4}{7} = 4$ **3** $\dfrac{a + 9}{4} = 6$ **4** $\dfrac{c}{5} - 3 = 2$ **5** $\dfrac{x - 8}{6} = 5$

6 $\dfrac{3n + 5}{2} = 3$ **7** $\dfrac{30}{x} = 5$ **8** $\dfrac{7}{a} = 2$ **9** $3 = \dfrac{11}{m}$

Copy and complete:

10 $\dfrac{20}{x + 3} = 5$

$20 = \boxed{}(x + 3)$

$20 = \boxed{} + \boxed{}$

$20 - \boxed{} = \boxed{}$

$\boxed{} = \boxed{}$

$x = \boxed{}$

11 $\dfrac{6 - 7n}{2n + 4} = -3$

$6 - 7n = -3(\boxed{} + \boxed{})$

$6 - 7n = \boxed{} - \boxed{}$

$6 + \boxed{} = \boxed{} + 7n$

$\boxed{} = \boxed{}$

$n = \boxed{}$

Solve the following equations

12 $\dfrac{15}{a + 1} = 3$

13 $\dfrac{21}{n - 2} = 7$

14 $\dfrac{10}{2y + 1} = 5$

15 $\dfrac{1 - 2m}{3} = 5$

16 $\dfrac{8}{w} + 3 = 7$

17 $\dfrac{5x + 7}{2x - 2} = 3$

18 $\dfrac{7f - 2}{3f - 1} = 5$

19 $\dfrac{3n + 2}{2n - 3} = 7$

20 $\dfrac{11z - 1}{5z - 2} = 3$

21 $\dfrac{6a - 1}{5a - 4} = 2$

22 $4 = \dfrac{6x + 5}{2x - 1}$

23 $\dfrac{7v + 3}{6v + 1} = 2$

TASK M6.4

1   **a** Write down an equation using the angles.
     b Find x.
     c Write down the actual value of each angle
       in this quadrilateral.

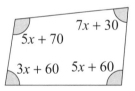

2 The length of a rectangle is 8 cm more than its width. If its perimeter is
44 cm, find its width.

3 Hannah has 3 times as much money as Joe. Hannah spends £24 on a
new blouse. She now has £30 left. How much money has Joe got?

4 This is an *isosceles* triangle.
    a Find the value of x.
    b Find the perimeter of the triangle.

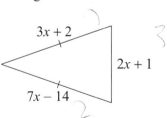

5 The area of this rectangle is 60 cm^2.
    a Write down an equation involving x.
    b Find x.

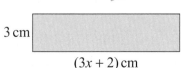

6 Three consecutive whole numbers add up to 144. If the lowest number is n,
   a Write down an expression for the other two numbers in terms of n.
   b Write down an equation involving n.
   c Find n then write down the three consecutive whole numbers.

7 The area of each rectangle is equal
   (all lengths are measured in cm).
   a Find the value of x.
   b Find the area of one of the rectangles.

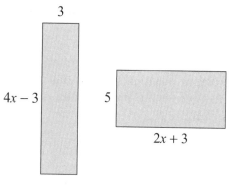

$4x - 3$

5

$2x + 3$

3

8 Find the actual length and width of this
   rectangle.

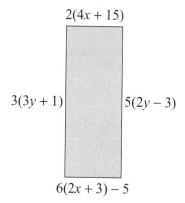

$2(4x + 15)$

$3(3y + 1)$

$5(2y - 3)$

$6(2x + 3) - 5$

TASK M6.5

1 The area of this rectangle is 42 cm².
   This means that $x(x + 4) = 42$
   Copy and complete the table below to find x to one decimal
   place by trial and improvement.

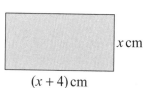

x cm

$(x + 4)$ cm

trial	calculation	too large or too small?
$x = 5$	$5 \times 9 = 45$	too large
$x = 4$	$4 \times 8 = 32$	too small
$x = 4·5$	$4·5 \times 8·5 = 38·25$	too ...
$x = 4·7$	$4·7 \times 8·7 = ...$	too ...
$x = 4·9$	$4·9 \times 8·9 = ...$	too ...
$x = 4·8$	$4·8 \times 8·8 = ...$	too ...
$x = 4·75$	$4·75 \times 8·75 = ...$	too ...
Answer: $x = ...$ (to one decimal place)		

2 Solve these equations by trial and improvement. Give each answer to
1 decimal place.

    a $x(x - 3) = 36$ **b** $x^2 + x = 77$

3 A cube of side length x has a hole
cut through it as shown.
A prism with end area equal to 3
and length x is removed.
The volume of the solid remaining is 140.
Form an equation and use trial and
improvement to find the value of x to
1 decimal place.

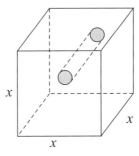

4 Solve these equations by trial and improvement. Give each answer to
2 decimal places.

    a $x^3 - x = 467$ **b** $x(x^2 + 5x) = 84$ **c** $4^x = 76$

TASK M6.6

1 $a = b - 10$ Make b the subject of the formula.

2 $n = 5m$ Make m the subject of the formula.

3 Write down the pairs of equations which belong to each other.

    A $y = 8x$ **B** $y = \frac{x}{8}$

    C $8y = x$ **D** $\frac{y}{8} = x$

4 Write down which working out below is correct.

    a $m = 4n + 8$ **b** $y = 2x - 6$

       $m + 8 = 4n$ $y + 6 = 2x$

       $\frac{m + 8}{4} = n$ $\frac{y + 6}{2} = x$

5 Make n the subject of each formula given below:

    a $m = cn - f$ **b** $x = gn + h$ **c** $an - 2m = y$

    d $m(n + p) = v$ **e** $x(n + f) = y$ **f** $h(n - 3) = x$

    g $y = \frac{n}{8} - 2$ **h** $q = w(n - p)$ **i** $\frac{n}{y} + f = 3g$

6 $\frac{an - b}{3} = c$ Make n the subject of the formula.

7 $\frac{mx + c}{a} = b$ Make x the subject of the formula.

8 $y = \frac{3(b + c)}{m}$ Make b the subject of the formula.

9 Make x the subject of each formula given below:

a $a(x + b) = c$ **b** $\dfrac{x + p}{q} = r$ **c** $\dfrac{p(x + q)}{r} = t$

d $\dfrac{h}{x} = u$ **e** $\dfrac{k}{x + b} = w$ **f** $\dfrac{d}{ax + b} = c$

10 Make w the subject of each formula given below:

a $a - bw = c$ **b** $\dfrac{p - qw}{r} = y$ **c** $h - \dfrac{w}{g} = k$

d $\dfrac{w + t}{m} = p - q$ **e** $b^2 - a(w + b) = c$ **f** $y = \dfrac{aw + b}{q} - c$

TASK M6.7

1 Copy and complete:

a $\sqrt{x} + b = a$

$\sqrt{x} = a - \square$

$x = (a - \square)^2$

b $\sqrt{(x + b)} = a$

$x + b = \square$

$x = \square - \square$

c $x^3 + w = 6m$

$x^3 = 6m - \square$

$x = \sqrt[\square]{(6m - \square)}$

2 Make x the subject of each formula given below:

a $x^2 + b = c$ **b** $px^2 + q = r$ **c** $ax^2 = b$

d $\dfrac{ax^2}{b} = c$ **e** $\sqrt{x} - m = w$ **f** $\dfrac{\sqrt{x} + u}{v} = z$

g $\dfrac{a\sqrt{x} + b}{c} = d$ **h** $a - x^3 = b$ **i** $\dfrac{\sqrt{(x - p)}}{t} = r$

3 $v^2 = u^2 + 2as$ Make u the subject of the formula.

4 $A = 4\pi r^3$ Make r the subject of the formula.

5 $w = up + 4aq^2$ Make a the subject of the formula.

6 $A = 8(w - p)^2$ Make w the subject of the formula.

7 Make n the subject of each formula given below:

a $h = \dfrac{m}{n}$ **b** $\dfrac{n}{v} - x = w$ **c** $h - \dfrac{n}{g} = k$

d $\dfrac{a}{n} + q = p$ **e** $\dfrac{b}{n + c} = m$ **f** $y = \dfrac{6a}{n - w}$

8 $\dfrac{h + a}{b} = \dfrac{x + d}{c}$ Make x the subject of the formula.

9 $T = \sqrt{\left(\dfrac{w - a}{g}\right)}$ Make w the subject of the formula.

10 Make y the subject of each formula given below:

a $\sqrt{\left(\dfrac{y}{m}\right)} = h$ **b** $\sqrt[3]{(y - z)} = r$ **c** $A = \dfrac{1}{2}my^3$

d $\sqrt[3]{(ay - b)} = c$ **e** $\sqrt{(my + n)} = p$ **f** $v - y^3 = a$

g $py^3 - q = x$ **h** $\sqrt{\left(\dfrac{y - m}{n}\right)} = w$ **i** $x = \dfrac{\sqrt[3]{(my + p)}}{3}$

TASK E6.1

1 Copy and complete:

a $ax - b = cx$
$ax - cx = \square$
$x(\square - \square) = \square$
$x = \dfrac{\square}{\square - \square}$

b $\dfrac{v + 3w}{v} = p$
$v + 3w = \square$
$3w = \square - \square$
$3w = v(\square - \square)$
$v = \dfrac{3w}{\square - \square}$

2 Make x the subject of each formula given below:

a $cx + f = mx$ **b** $mx - w = px$
c $ax + b = cx + d$ **d** $a(x - c) = b(x + f)$
e $4x = m(x + y)$ **f** $p + qx = m(n - x)$

3 Make x the subject of the formula $a = \dfrac{c + bx}{x}$

4 Make m the subject of the formula $m = \dfrac{d + em}{a}$

5 Make w the subject of the formula $\dfrac{aw}{w + b} = c$

6 Make v the subject of the formula $\dfrac{p - qv}{r - sv} = t$

7 Make q the subject of the formula $\dfrac{kq}{q + b} = e$

8 Make n the subject of each formula given below:

a $\sqrt{\dfrac{a - bn}{n}} = c$ **b** $\sqrt{\dfrac{n - 1}{n}} = t$ **c** $b = \sqrt[3]{\dfrac{n}{n + a}}$

d $\left(\dfrac{n - c}{n}\right)^2 = a$ **e** $y = \left(\dfrac{m + n}{n}\right)^3$ **f** $\sqrt{\dfrac{n - w}{n - x}} = p$

9 $\dfrac{aw + y}{c} = \dfrac{bw + u}{d}$ Make w the subject of the formula.

10 $P = \dfrac{1}{x}\left(\dfrac{WQ}{R} - M\right)$ Make R the subject of the formula.

TASK E6.2

1 If $f(x) = 3x + 6$, find the value of:
   a $f(z)$ **b** $f(-4)$ **c** $f(-1)$ **d** $f(200)$

2 If $g(x) = x^3$, find the value of:
   a $g(3)$ **b** $g(-1)$ **c** $g(-4)$ **d** $g\left(\dfrac{1}{2}\right)$

3 If $h(x) = (x + 3)^2$, find the value of:
   a $h(4)$ **b** $h(0)$ **c** $h(-2)$ **d** $h(p)$

4 If $f(x) = \dfrac{x^2 + 3x - 1}{x + 4}$, find the value of:
   a $f(0)$ **b** $f(1)$ **c** $f(-1)$ **d** $f(w)$

5 If $f(x) = 2x + 7$, find the value of x when $f(x) = 23$.

6 If $g(x) = 4x - 18$, find the value of x when $g(x) = -26$.

7 If $h(x) = \dfrac{5 - 3x}{7}$, find the value of x when $h(x) = -4$.

8 If $g(x) = x^2 - 3x$, find the values of x when $g(x) = 18$.

9 If $f(x) = x^2 + 8$, find the values of w when $f(w) = 6w$.

10 If $f(x) = 14$, find the value(s) of x when
   a $f(x) = 20 - 2x$ **b** $f(x) = x^2 - 5x$ **c** $f(x) = x^2 - 8x + 14$

11 If $g(x) = 3x + 2$, write down each function below:
   a $g(x) - 6$ **b** $4g(x) + 1$ **c** $5 - g(x)$ **d** $2 - 6g(x)$

12 If $f(x) = 5x - 3$ and $g(x) = 2x + 9$, solve $f(x) + 4 = 3 - g(x)$

13 If $f(x) = 4\underset{\underline{\quad}\uparrow}{x} + 5$ then $f(x - 3) = 4(\underset{\underline{\quad}\uparrow}{x} - 3) + 5 = 4x - 7$

   Write down the function $f(2x + 1)$.

14 If $g(x) = 3x - 6$, write down each function below:
   a $g(x + 4)$ **b** $g(2x)$ **c** $g(-x)$

TASK M6.8

1 **a** Write down the equation of the line which
       passes through P and R.
   b Write down the equation of the line which
       passes through S and U.
   c Write down the equation of the line which
       passes through P and Q.
   d Write down the equation of the line which
       passes through W, Q and V.

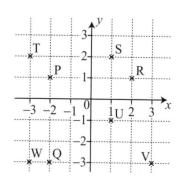

2 Using x-values from 0 to 4, complete a table then draw the straight line $y = 4x + 1$ (make sure you draw the axes big enough).

3 Copy and complete the table below then draw the straight line $y = 4 - x$.

x	0	1	2	3
y				

4 Using x-values from -3 to 3, complete a table then draw the straight line $y = 2x + 3$.

5 Draw $y = 5 - 4x$ using x-values from -2 to 2.

TASK M6.9

1 Copy and complete the table below then draw the curve $y = x^2 + 2$.

x	-3	-2	-1	0	1	2	3
y							

2 Copy and complete the table below then draw the curve $y = 4x^2$.

x	-2	-1	0	1	2
y					

3 a Copy and complete the table below then draw the curve $y = x^2 + 4x$.

x	-5	-4	-3	-2	-1	0	1	2
x^2				4				4
$+4x$				-8				8
y				-4				12

   b Read off the x-values from the graph when $y = 2$.

4 a Copy and complete the table below then draw the curve $y = x^2 + 5x - 4$.

x	-5	-4	-3	-2	-1	0	1	2
x^2	25							
$+5x$	-25							
-4	-4	-4	-4					
y	-4							

   b Use the graph to estimate the y-value when $x = -3 \cdot 5$.
   c Use the graph to estimate the x-values when $y = -6$.

5 **a** Draw the graph of $y = 2x^2 - x + 5$ for x-values from -3 to 3.
   b Use the graph to estimate the x-values when $y = 8$.

TASK E6.3

1 **a** Copy and complete the table below then draw the curve
   $y = x^3 - 2x + 1$.

x	-3	-2	-1	0	1	2	3
x^3		-8					
$-2x$		$+4$					
$+1$	$+1$	$+1$					
y		-3					

   b Use the graph to estimate the x-values when $y = 1{\cdot}5$.

2 **a** Draw the graph of $y = x^3 - 2x^2 + 3$ for x-values from -2 to 4.
   b Use the graph to estimate the x-value when $y = 10$.

3 **a** Draw the graph of $y = \dfrac{20}{x - 1}$ for x-values from -4 to 6 (Be careful
   when $x = 1$).
   b Use the graph to estimate the x-value when $y = -8$.

4

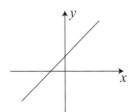

1.

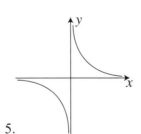

2.

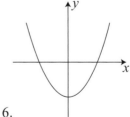

3.

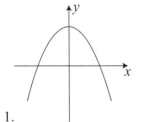

4.

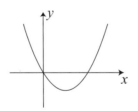

5.

6.

Match each equation to its graph above. One of the equations does not
have a graph above.

A $y = \dfrac{5}{x}$ **B** $y = x^2 - 10$ **C** $y = x^2 - x$ **D** $y = 1 - 4x$

E $y = 6 - x^2$ **F** $y = 5 + 7x - x^3$ **G** $y = 4x + 1$

TASK E6.4

1 Copy these axes and sketch the graph of a car travelling at a steady speed then accelerating rapidly.

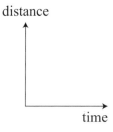

2

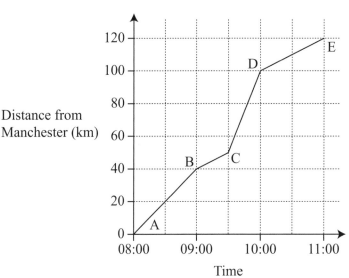

The graph above shows a car journey from Manchester.
a How far from Manchester is the car at 10:30?
b When is the car half way between B and C?
c At what time is the car 30 km from Manchester?
d Find the speed (in km/h) of the car from B to C.
e Find the speed (in km/h) of the car from C to D.

3 The pressure P of a quantity of gas is given by the formula $P = \dfrac{50}{V}$
where V is the volume.
a Draw a graph of P against V for values of V from 1 to 8.
b Use the graph to find the value of P when $V = 3.5$.
c Use the graph to find the value of V when $P = 11$.

4 The volume of this *open box* is 10 cm^3.
a Prove that $h = \dfrac{10}{w^2}$
b Prove that the surface area A is given by
$A = \dfrac{40}{w} + w^2$
c Draw a graph of A against w for values of w from 1 to 5.
d What is the minimum possible surface area?
e What value of w will give this minimum surface area?

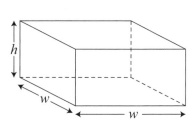

TASK M6.10

1 Find the gradient of each line below:

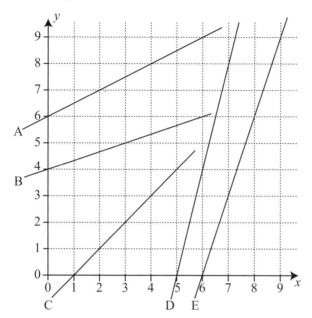

Remember:
Gradient =
$$\frac{\text{vertical distance}}{\text{horizontal distance}}$$

2 Find the gradient of each line below:

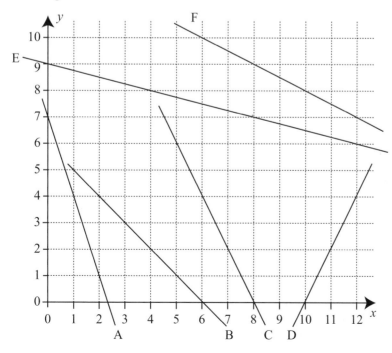

3 Find the gradient of the line joining each pair of points below:

    a $(2, 4)$ and $(3, 7)$ **b** $(1, 0)$ and $(4, 5)$ **c** $(1, 4)$ and $(3, 2)$

    d $(1, 5)$ and $(5, 2)$ **e** $(-3, -2)$ and $(1, -10)$ **f** $(4, -1)$ and $(6, -4)$

4 A line passes through the points $(2, 6)$ and $(5, y)$. If the gradient of the line is -3, write down the value of y.

5 Find the gradient of each line below (look at the numbers on the axes very carefully):

a 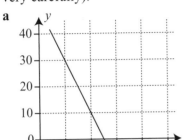   **b**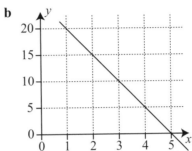

TASK M6.11

1 The equation of each line is shown below:

    (A) $y = -2x + 6$ (B) $y = -2x + 2$

    (C) $y = -2x$ (D) $y = -2x - 3$

    a Use the graph to find the gradient of lines (A), (B), (C) and (D).

    b What do you notice about the gradient of each line and its equation?

    c Look at where each line cuts the y-axis. For each line, what do you notice about this value and its equation?

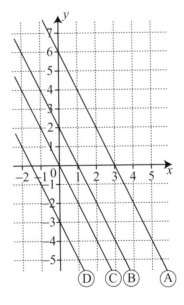

2 **a** Draw the following lines using the same set of axes:

       $y = 3x + 4$ $y = 3x + 1$ $y = 3x$ $y = 3x - 2$ $y = 3x - 3$

    b Find the gradient of each line. What do you notice about the gradient of each line and its equation?

    c Look at where each line cuts the y-axis. For each line, what do you notice about this value and its equation?

TASK M6.12

1 Which lines below are parallel?

$y = 5x + 1$ $y = 3x + 1$ $y = 1 - 5x$ $y = 5x + 4$ $y = 3 + 5x$

2 Which lines below cut the y-axis at the same point?

$y = 3x + 2$ $y = 2 + 4x$ $y = 3x - 2$ $y = 2x + 3$ $y = 2x$

3 Write down **i** the gradient and **ii** the y-intercept of each line below:

  a $y = 8x + 4$ **b** $y = 2x - 6$ **c** $y = x$ **d** $y = x - 5$

  e $y = 4 - 2x$ **f** $y = \frac{1}{4}x + 3$ **g** $y + 3x = 2$ **h** $7x - y = 6$

  i $2y - 4x = 6$ **j** $3y + 2x = 1$ **k** $5x + 2y = 7$ **l** $4x - 5y - 3 = 0$

4 Write down the equation of each of the 3 lines shown.

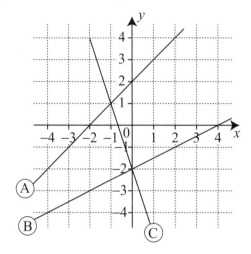

5 Find the equation of the straight line which passes through $(0, 5)$ and has a gradient of 6.

6 Find the equation of the straight line which passes through $(1, 5)$ and has a gradient of 2.

7 Write down the equation of each line shown below:

a

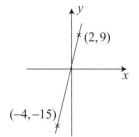

b

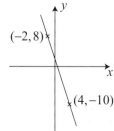

8 Find the equation of the straight line which passes through $(-6, 12)$ and $(2, 8)$.

TASK E6.5

1 Draw an *x*-axis from −8 to 8 and a *y*-axis from −8 to 8.
   a Draw $y = x - 1$
   b Draw the line perpendicular to $y = x - 1$ which has the same *y*-intercept.
   c Find the equation of the line drawn in part **b**.
   d *Multiply* together the gradients of the 2 lines you have drawn.

2 Draw an *x*-axis from −8 to 8 and a *y*-axis from −8 to 8.
   a Draw $y = 2x + 1$
   b Draw the line perpendicular to $y = 2x + 1$ which passes through (2, 5).
   c Find the equation of the line drawn in part **b**.
   d *Multiply* together the gradients of the 2 lines you have drawn.

3 **a** If the gradient of the line $y = 5x + 3$ is multiplied by the gradient of a line perpendicular to $y = 5x + 3$, what number would be obtained?
   b Write down the gradient of a line which is perpendicular to $y = 5x + 3$.

TASK E6.6

1 Write down the gradient of the line which is perpendicular to a line with each gradient given below:
   a 4   **b** 9   **c** −2   **d** 6   **e** −1   **f** $\frac{1}{5}$

   g $\frac{3}{7}$ **h** $\frac{-1}{3}$ **i** $\frac{-2}{5}$ **j** −0·25   **k** 0·1   **l** $\frac{13}{5}$

2 Write down the gradient of any line which is perpendicular to each line shown below:

a

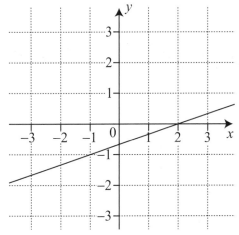

b

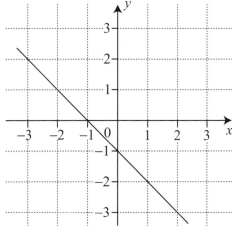

   c Write down the equation of the line which is perpendicular to the line shown in part **a** and passes through $(0, 2)$.

   d Write down the equation of the line which is perpendicular to the line shown in part **b** and has the same y-intercept.

3 A line passes through $(0, -3)$ and is perpendicular to the line $y = 4x + 3$. Find the equation of the line.

4 A line passes through $(2, 13)$ and is perpendicular to the line $y = -\frac{1}{2}x + 5$. Find the equation of the line.

5 A line passes through $(3, 11)$ and is *parallel* to the line $y = 3x - 4$. Find the equation of the line.

6 Which of the lines below are perpendicular to the line $3x + y = 4$?

$x - 3y = 6$	$y = 3x - 2$	$x + 3y = 1$	$y = 1 - 3x$	$y = \frac{1}{3}x + 5$

7 Find the equation of the line which passes through the given point and is perpendicular to the given line.

   a $(1, 11)$ $x + 6y = 6$ **b** $(3, 8)$ $x + 3y = 12$

   c $(6, 7)$ **d** $(-3, -3)$

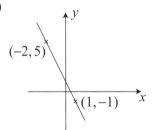

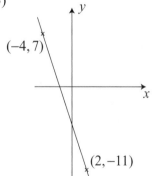

DATA 1   **8**

TASK M8.1

1 Freddie throws a coin 120 times. The coin lands on 'tails' 58 times.

   a From Freddie's results, find the *relative frequency* of getting 'tails'.

$$\left(\text{relative frequency} = \frac{\text{number of times event happens}}{\text{total number of trials}}\right)$$

   b Do you think the coin is fair? *Explain* the answer you give.

2 Jo is throwing an 8-sided dice. She throws the dice 240 times.
The table below shows her results.

score	1	2	3	4	5	6	7	8
frequency	27	24	36	27	30	27	33	36

a How many times should each number come up if the dice is fair?
b From Jo's results, *use a calculator* to find the relative frequency
of getting each score (1 up to 8).
c Do you think the dice is fair? *Explain* the answer you give.

3 Mary keeps throwing a drawing pin to find out how many times it
will land 'point down'. The table below shows the total number of times
the drawing pin has landed 'point down' after every 20 throws.

number of throws	20	40	60	80	100	120	140	160	180	200
number of 'point down'	5	13	21	26	36	47	53	59	68	76

a Work out the relative frequency of the drawing pin landing 'point down'
after every 20 throws (round off to 2 decimal places if necessary).
b Plot a graph of the relative frequency of 'point down' against the
total number of throws.
c Write down the number around which the relative frequency of
'point down' is settling.

4 Five people throw a biased dice several times. They record how many
times the dice lands on a '2'.

Name	Number of throws	Number of 2's	Relative frequency
Helena	100	41	0·41
Sandeep	200	83	0·415
Rory	150	60	0·4
Natalie	450	99	0·22
Ben	700	273	0·39

One of these five people made a mistake when recording the number of
2's. Who do you think this was? Give a reason for your answer.

TASK M8.2

1 Sue has 15 cards as shown below:

Sue picks a card at random.
What is the probability that she picks the letter:
a C **b** E **c** L **d** S

2 Angus has a bag which contains 7 toffees, 4 mints and 2 chocolates.
Angus picks one of these sweets.
What is the probability that he chooses a:

a mint   **b** mint or toffee   **c** mint or chocolate

3 A bag contains 10 beads. There are 6 blue,
3 red and 1 green.

a Find the probability of selecting a red bead.

b 2 more blue beads are put in the bag.
Find the probability of selecting a blue bead.

4 24 people come for a job interview. 9 of these people wear glasses and
4 of them have contact lenses.
Find the probability that the person chosen for the job:

a has contact lenses

b wears glasses

c does not wear glasses or contact lenses

5 Wendy has six £5 notes, ten £10 notes and four £20 notes in her purse.
If she takes out one note, what is the probability that it will be:

a a £20 note   **b** a £5 or £10 note   **c** a £50 note

d She buys a new toaster with a £20 note and a £10 note.
If she now took out a note, what is the probability that
it would be a £10 note?

6 Reuben throws an 8-sided dice (faces numbered from 1 to 8) once.
What is the probability of getting:

a a multiple of 2   **b** a prime number   **c** a factor of 8

7 One night a kennel has 16 dogs and 7 cats in its care. The following
morning 3 dogs and 4 cats are picked up by their owners and 2 dogs are
dropped off at the kennel.
Another owner arrives. What is the probability that if the owner has
come to pick up one pet only, it will be a cat?

8 One ball is selected from a bag containing x red balls, y blue balls
and z yellow balls. What is the probability of selecting a blue ball?

9 A box contains n beads. 8 beads are blue, m beads are green and the
remaining beads are yellow. If one bead is removed, what is the
probability that it will be yellow?

10 A bag contains x balls. y balls are removed and z balls are added.
6 balls are white. If one white ball is removed, what is the probability
that the next ball to be removed will *not* be white?

TASK M8.3

1 A coin is thrown 48 times. How many times would you expect it to land on 'heads'?

2 A dice is thrown 120 times.
How many times would you expect to get a:
   a 3   **b** 5   **c** 4 or 5   **d** square number

3 This spinner is spun 80 times.
How many times should the spinner
land on a '0'?

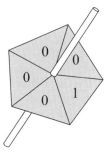

4 The probability of Canning Albion winning a football match is $\frac{2}{3}$.
If they play 42 matches in a season, how many matches are they likely to win?

5 The probability of Rob going to the pub on any one day is $\frac{2}{7}$. How many times is he likely to go to the pub in the next fortnight?

6 A bag contains 5 blue balls, 4 red balls and 1 yellow ball.
Brenda takes out one ball at random and then puts it back.
If she does this 70 times, how many times would she take out:
   a a yellow ball   **b** a blue ball   **c** a blue or red ball

7 The probability of Manchester United winning the Premiership during a season is 0·17. How many times are Manchester United likely to win the Premiership during the 21st. century?

8 A bag has only red and blue discs in it. The probability of picking red is $\frac{2}{5}$.
   a What is the probability of picking a blue disc?
   b Sam picks out 4 red discs without replacing them. What is the smallest number of blue discs that could have been in the bag?
   c If Sam picks out a total of 6 red discs without replacing them, what is the smallest number of blue discs that could have been in the bag?

TASK M8.4

1 Here are 2 spinners. If I spin both spinners, I could get a
'1' and a '4' (1, 4).

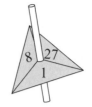 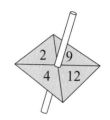

  a List *all* the possible outcomes.
  b How many possible outcomes are there?

2 Three babies are born. List *all* the boy/girl mixes (example: B G B
boy, girl, boy).

3 Bart has 4 films (Antz, King Kong, Jungle Book and The Terminator).
He only has time to watch two of the films. List *all* the possible pairs
of films that he could watch.

4 Nina has 2 spinners. She spins both spinners and
multiplies the numbers. For example a '3' and a
'4' give 12.

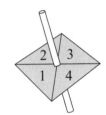

  a Copy and complete this grid to show *all*
     the possible outcomes.
Find the probability of getting a product which is:
  b an odd number
  c less than 3
  d a prime number

X	1	2	3	4
1				
2				
3				12
4				

5

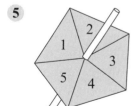

Marie and Don play a game
involving a spinner
and a dice.

Marie wins if the spinner gives a square number and the dice gives
a multiple of 3.
Don wins if the spinner gives an even number and the dice gives
a factor of 15.
Any other outcome is a draw.
Is this game fair to both players? Give reasons for your answer.

TASK M8.5

1 The probability of Sean getting up before 11 a.m. on a Saturday morning is $\frac{1}{4}$. What is the probability of Sean *not* getting up before 11 a.m. on a Saturday morning?

2 The players in an amateur football team have the jobs shown below:

team position	job
goalkeeper	plumber
defenders	teacher, farmer, mechanic, artist
midfielders	farmer, fireman, insurance salesman
forwards	electrician, teacher, bus driver

Which of the following pairs are mutually exclusive?
a a teacher and a midfielder
b a farmer and a defender
c an electrician and a forward

3 The probability of Karen playing certain sports is shown in the table below.

hockey	football	badminton	netball
0·5	0·1	x	0·2

a What is the probability of Karen playing hockey or netball?
b What is the probability of Karen playing badminton?

4 The probability of picking a picture card from a pack of cards is $\frac{3}{13}$. What is the probability of *not* picking a picture card?

5 If the probability of England winning the next football World Cup is 0·15, what is the probability of England *not* winning the next World Cup?

6 Dan gets to work by either car, bus, tube or bike. The table shows the probability of each being used.

car	bus	tube	bike
0·25		0·4	0·2

a What is the probability of Dan going to work by bus.
b What is the probability of Dan going to work by car or bus.
c On his 20 working days in March, how many days would you expect Dan to take the tube?

7　There are 4 people in a car. One person is wearing glasses. 2 people are wearing hats. *Explain* why the probability of a person in the car wearing glasses or a hat is *not* necessarily $\frac{3}{4}$.

8　John has some coins in his pocket. He has £1, £2 and 50p coins. The probability of choosing a £1 coin is 0·65. The probability of choosing a £2 coin is 0·2.
  a　What is the probability of choosing a 50p coin?
  b　What is the probability of choosing a £2 coin or a 50p coin?

TASK M8.6

1　A coin is thrown twice. What is the probability of getting 2 heads?

2　A dice is thrown twice. What is the probability of getting a '3' *followed* by a '4'?

3　A card is taken from a pack of 52 playing cards then replaced. Another card is chosen. What is the probability of obtaining:
  a　2 diamond cards?
  b　2 aces?

4　A bag contains 6 yellow beads, 3 blue beads and 2 green beads.
I remove one bead at random, replace it then take another bead.
What is the probability that:
  a　both beads are blue?
  b　both beads are green?

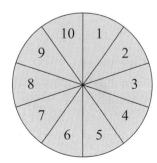

5　The probability that Will takes an umbrella to work is 0·4.
The probability that it rains is 0·7.
What is the probability that:
  a　Will takes his umbrella and it rains?
  b　Will does *not* take his umbrella and it rains?
  c　Will does *not* take his umbrella and it does *not* rain?

6　2 darts are thrown at this board.
Assuming each dart hits the board, what is the probability that:
  a　both darts hit an even number?
  b　both darts hit a square number?
  c　both darts hit a prime number?

7 If a dice is thrown four times, what is the probability of obtaining four sixes?

8 The probability that Serena works on a Saturday is $\frac{3}{4}$. The probability that she goes to a night club on a Saturday evening is $\frac{4}{7}$.

On any Saturday what is the probability that:
a Serena does *not* work but goes to a night club?
b Serena works and goes to a night club?

TASK M8.7

1 A bag contains 8 blue discs and 3 green discs. One disc is removed at random then replaced. Another disc is then removed.
a Copy and complete the tree diagram to show all the outcomes.
Find the probability that:
b both discs are blue
c both discs are green
d one disc is blue and one disc is green (in any order)

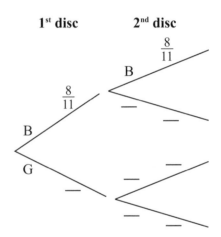

2 The probability of Jack swimming on any one day is 0·3.
a Copy and complete the tree diagram showing whether he swims or not on a Thursday and Friday.
b Find the probability that:
    i Jack does *not* swim on either day
    ii Jack swims on one day *only*

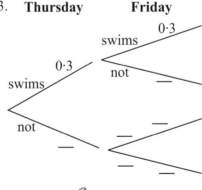

3 A spinner is spun three times.
a Copy and complete the tree diagram to show the probability of getting a 'two'.

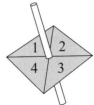

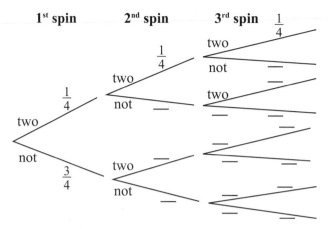

b Find the probability that the spinner lands on:
   i   3 two's
   ii no two's
   iii *at least* one 'two'

4 A dice is thrown three times. Find the probability that the dice
lands on:
a exactly two 3's
b *at least* one 3

5 The probability of Stacey eating a curry on any day is 0·2.
Draw a tree diagram to help you find the probability that on a Friday,
Saturday and Sunday:
a Stacey has a curry each day
b Stacey has a curry on exactly one day only
c Stacey has a curry on *at least* one day

TASK E8.1

1 There are 3 males and 5 females in a family of
8 people. Two of the family members are
chosen at random.
a Copy and complete the tree diagram.
Find the probability that:
b both people are female
c exactly one person is female

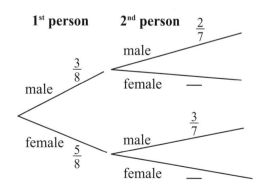

2 Charlie has 7 creme eggs and 2 caramel eggs. He eats 2 eggs randomly.
   a Draw a tree diagram to show all outcomes.
   Find the probability that:
   b Charlie eats 2 creme eggs
   c Charlie eats one creme egg and one caramel egg
   d Charlie eats 2 eggs of the same type

3 Three cards are taken at random from
   a pack of 52 cards.
   a Copy and complete the tree diagram.
   b Find the probability that:
      i all 3 cards are clubs
      ii *at least* one card is a club
      iii exactly one card is a club

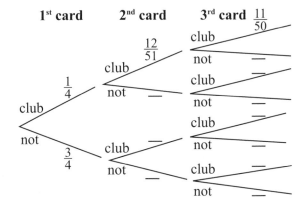

4 There are 12 beads in a bag. 5 beads are red and the rest are blue.
   Three beads are taken out at random, one at a time, without replacement.
   a Draw a tree to show all outcomes.
   Find the probability that:
   b all three beads are blue
   c *at least* one bead is red
   d exactly one bead is blue and two beads are red

5 A box contains 15 counters. x counters are red and the remainder
   are blue. Two counters are removed at random. What is the
   probability, in terms of x, of removing:
   a two blue counters?
   b *at least* one blue counter?
   c one counter of each colour?

TASK E8.2

1 The probability of a garden gate being left open is 0.15. If the gate
   is left open, the probability of a dog getting out of the garden is 0.8.
   If the gate is shut, the probability of the dog getting out of the garden
   is 0.3.
   a Copy and complete the tree diagram.
   b Find the probability that the dog gets out of the garden.

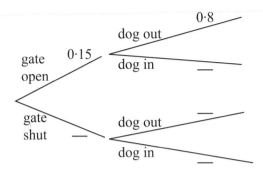

2 The probability of Amy doing more than 2 hours homework on a
   Thursday evening is 0·6. If she does more than 2 hours homework, the
   probability of seeing friends later that evening is 0·25. If she does
   2 hours or less homework, the probability of seeing friends later that
   evening is 0·7.
   a Draw a tree diagram to represent the above information.
   b Find the probability that Amy will see friends later
        that evening.

3 65% of properties for sale in a town are over-priced. If a property is
   over-priced, the probability of getting the asking price is 0·3. If the
   property is not over-priced, the probability of getting the asking price
   is 0·85.
   a Draw a tree diagram to represent the above information.
   b Find the probability of not receiving the asking price.

4 A rugby team plays 40% of its matches at home. They win 75% of their
   home matches but only 55% of their away matches.
   a Draw a tree diagram to represent the above information.
   b Find the probability that the team wins a match.

5 If a car salesperson sells more than 3 cars during the week, the
   probability of taking the next weekend off is $\frac{7}{8}$. If 3 or less cars are sold
   during the week, the probability of taking the next weekend off is $\frac{2}{5}$.
   If the probability of selling more than 3 cars during the week is $\frac{1}{5}$,
   find the probability that the car salesperson will take the next
   weekend off.

6 A bag contains n counters. Seven of these counters are green and the
   rest are yellow. Two counters are chosen at random. The probability
   that the two counters are green is $\frac{1}{5}$.
   a Form an equation involving n and show that it simplifies to
        $n^2 - n - 210 = 0$.
   b Find how many counters were in the bag originally.

SHAPE 2   9

TASK M9.1

1 Copy the patterns below on squared paper. Shade in as many squares as necessary to complete the symmetrical patterns. The dotted lines are lines of symmetry.

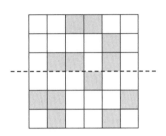 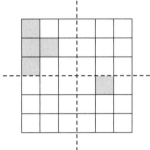

2 Sketch these shapes in your book and draw on *all* the *lines of symmetry.*

For each shape write the *order* of *rotational symmetry* (you may use tracing paper).

3    **4** 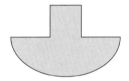   **5** 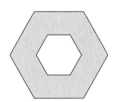   **6**

7   **8**    **9** 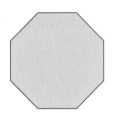   **10**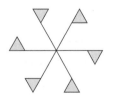

11 Draw your own shape which has an order of rotational symmetry of 3.

12 Draw a triangle which has *no* rotational symmetry.

TASK M9.2

1 How many planes of symmetry does this triangular prism have?

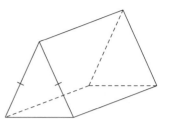

2 Draw each shape below and show one plane of symmetry.

a

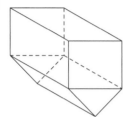

b

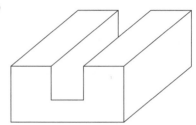

c

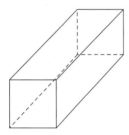

d

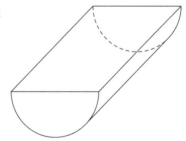

3 How may planes of symmetry does a cube have?

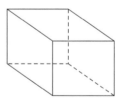

TASK M9.3

1 Use translation vectors to describe the following translations.

a	D to C	**b**	E to D
c	A to B	**d**	E to F
e	D to H	**f**	H to F
g	E to B	**h**	E to G
i	G to D	**j**	F to C

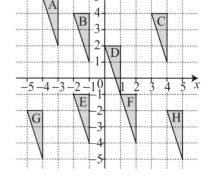

68

2 Copy the grid opposite and draw shape A as shown.
Translate shape A by each of the translation vectors
shown below:

a $\begin{pmatrix} -4 \\ 1 \end{pmatrix}$ Label new shape B.

b $\begin{pmatrix} 1 \\ -3 \end{pmatrix}$ Label new shape C.

c $\begin{pmatrix} -4 \\ -3 \end{pmatrix}$ Label new shape D.

d $\begin{pmatrix} -1 \\ -5 \end{pmatrix}$ Label new shape E.

e Use a translation vector to describe the translation
that moves shape D to E.

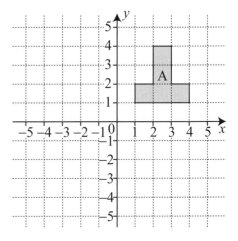

TASK M9.4

1 For each pair of shapes below, write down the
name of the *line of reflection*.
  a A to B
  b A to C
  c C to D
  d D to E
  e E to F

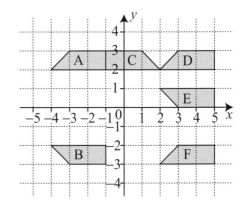

2 Copy the grid and shape opposite.
  a Reflect rectangle A in the line $y = x - 1$.
  Label the image B.
  b Draw the line $y = -x$.
  c Reflect rectangle A in the line $y = -x$.
  Label the image C.
  d Write down the translation vector which
  transforms rectangle C onto rectangle B.

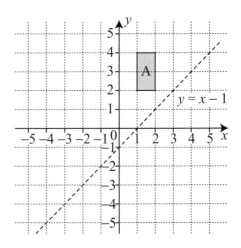

3   **a**   Draw an *x*-axis from −4 to 6 and a *y*-axis from −4 to 6.

     b   Draw a triangle P with vertices (1, 3), (1, 6) and (2, 3).

     c   Reflect triangle P in the line $y = x$. Label the image Q.

     d   Reflect triangle Q in the line $x + y = 3$. Label the image R.

     e   Reflect triangle R in the line $x = -1$. Label the image S.

     f   Reflect triangle S in the *x*-axis. Label the image T.

     g   Describe fully the transformation which maps T back onto P.

4   **a**   Draw an *x*-axis from −5 to 5 and a *y*-axis from −5 to 5.

     b   Draw an ⌐-shape A with vertices (−2, 1), (−2, 4), (−4, 4),

        (−4, 3), (−3, 3) and (−3, 1).

     c   Translate shape A through $\begin{pmatrix} 3 \\ 0 \end{pmatrix}$. Label the image B.

     d   Reflect shape B in the line $y = x$. Label the image C.

     e   Translate shape C through $\begin{pmatrix} -1 \\ -2 \end{pmatrix}$. Label the image D.

     f   Shape D is reflected back onto shape A. Write down the equation of
the *line of reflection*.

TASK M9.5

You may use tracing paper.

For each Question, draw the shape and the centre of rotation (C). Rotate
the image as indicated and draw the image.

1 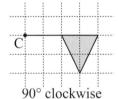   **2**   **3** 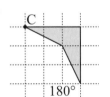   **4**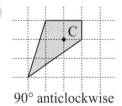

     90° clockwise   90° anticlockwise   180°   90° anticlockwise

5   Find the co-ordinates of the centres of the
following rotations:

    a   shape A onto shape B

    b   shape B onto shape C

    c   shape C onto shape D

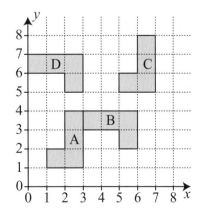

6 **a** Draw the *x* axis from −6 to 5.
Draw the *y* axis from −6 to 7.
Draw rectangle A with vertices at (2, −2), (3, −2), (3, −5), (2, −5).
b Rotate rectangle A 90° clockwise about (2, −1). Label the image B.
c Rotate rectangle B 90° clockwise about (−2, −2). Label the image C.
d Rotate rectangle C 90° clockwise about the origin. Label the image D.
e Rotate rectangle D 90° anticlockwise about (−2, 2). Label the image E.
f Describe *fully* the *translation* which transforms rectangle A onto rectangle E.

7 Describe *fully* the rotation which transforms:
a triangle A onto triangle B
b triangle C onto triangle D
c triangle B onto triangle C

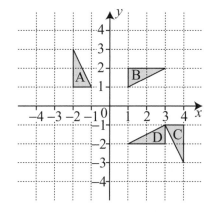

TASK M9.6

For Questions **1** and **2**, draw the grid and the 2 shapes then draw broken lines through pairs of points in the new shape and the old shape. Describe *fully* the enlargement which transforms shape A onto shape B.

1

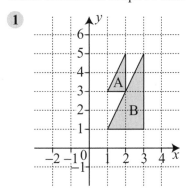

2

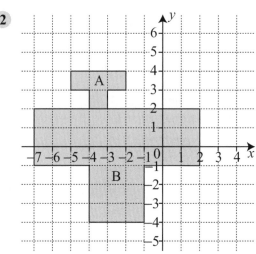

For Questions ③ to ⑤, copy the diagram and then draw an enlargement using the scale factor and centre of enlargement (C) given.
Leave room for the enlargement!

3

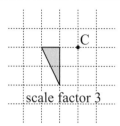

scale factor 3

4

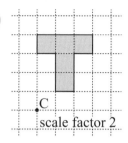

C
scale factor 2

5

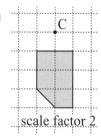

scale factor 2

6 **a** Draw an x-axis from −7 to 7 and a y-axis from −7 to 7.
   b Draw a rectangle P with vertices at (−1, −2), (−1, −3), (−3, −3) and (−3, −2).
   c Enlarge rectangle P by scale factor 2 about (0, 0). Label the image Q.
   d Translate rectangle Q through $\begin{pmatrix} 8 \\ 3 \end{pmatrix}$. Label the image R.
   e Enlarge rectangle R by scale factor 2 about (6, −7). Label the image S.
   f Enlarge rectangle S by scale factor $\frac{1}{4}$ about (−6, 5). Label the image T.
   g Describe fully the transformation which maps T onto P.

TASK E9.1

1 **a** Draw an x-axis from −5 to 5 and a y-axis from −5 to 5.
   b Draw an ⌐-shape with vertices at (−4, 2), (−4, 3), (−3, 3), (−3, 4), (−5, 4) and (−5, 2).
   c Enlarge the shape by a scale factor of −2 about (−2, 1).
   d If P is the vertex (−5, 2) in the original shape, write down the co-ordinates of the corresponding vertex in the new shape.

For Questions **2** and **3**, describe fully the enlargement which transforms shape A onto shape B (draw the grid and shape if necessary).

2

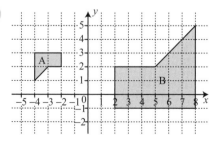

3

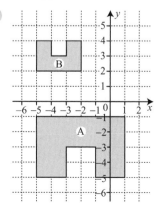

4 **a** Draw an *x*-axis from −6 to 4 and a *y*-axis from −10 to 4.
   b Draw a triangle A with vertices at (1, 1), (1, 3) and (2, 1).
   c Enlarge triangle A by a scale factor of −3 about the origin. Label the image B.
   d Enlarge triangle B by a scale factor of −$\frac{1}{3}$ about (0, −3). Label the image C.
   e Describe fully the transformation which maps C onto A.

TASK E9.2

1 Describe *fully* the transformation which moves:
   a triangle A onto triangle B
   b triangle B onto triangle C
   c triangle C onto triangle D
   d triangle D onto triangle E
   e triangle D onto triangle F

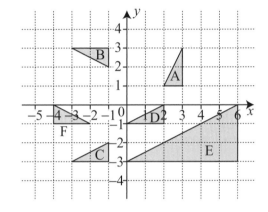

2 **a** Draw the *x*-axis from −5 to 5.
        Draw the *y*-axis from −6 to 6.
        Draw shape A with vertices at (−2, 2), (−4, 2), (−4, 4), (−2, 6).
   b Enlarge shape A by scale factor $\frac{1}{2}$ about the origin. Label the image B.
   c Reflect shape B in the line *y* = −1. Label the image C.
   d Rotate shape C 90° anticlockwise about (−2, −2). Label the image D.
   e Translate shape D through $\begin{pmatrix} 3 \\ 4 \end{pmatrix}$. Label the image E.
   f Rotate shape E 90° clockwise about (2, 2). Label the image F.
   g Describe *fully* the transformation that would move shape F onto shape C.

3 **a** Draw an *x*-axis from −7 to 7 and a *y*-axis from −7 to 7.
   b Draw rectangle P with vertices at (−4, −2), (−4, −6), (−6, −6) and (−6, −2).
   c Enlarge rectangle P by a scale factor of −$\frac{1}{2}$ about the origin. Label the image Q.
   d Reflect rectangle Q in the line *x* + *y* = 6. Label the image R.
   e Rotate rectangle R 90° clockwise about the origin. Label the image S.
   f Translate rectangle S through $\begin{pmatrix} -10 \\ 6 \end{pmatrix}$. Label the image T.
   g Describe fully the transformation which maps T onto Q.

TASK E9.3

1 *Explain* why these two triangles are congruent.

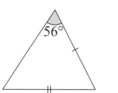 

2 *Explain* why these two triangles are *not* congruent.

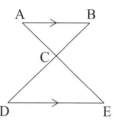

3 AB is parallel to DE.
BC = CD.
Prove that triangles ABC and CDE are congruent.

4 **a** Prove that triangles ACX and ACY are congruent.
b *Explain* why AY = CX.

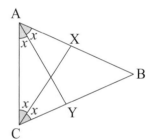

5 ABCD is a parallelogram.
Prove that triangles ABD and CBD are congruent.

6 PR = RS.
Prove that triangles PQR and RTS are congruent.

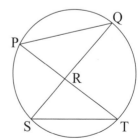

7 Triangle BCE is isosceles as shown.
AB = ED.
a Prove that triangles ABC and CED are congruent.
b *Explain* why ∠BAC = ∠CDE.

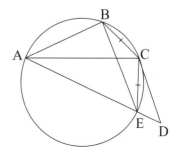

8 PQRS is a kite.
Use congruent triangles to prove that diagonal
PR bisects ∠SPQ.

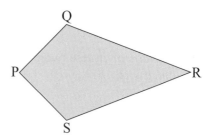

9 Triangle ABC is isosceles with AB = BC.
M and N are the midpoints of AB and BC
respectively.
PQBM and BRSN are both squares.
   a Prove that triangles BRM and BNQ are
   congruent.
   b Explain why MR = NQ.

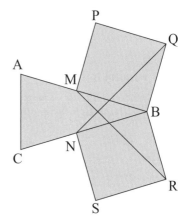

SHAPE 3   10

TASK M10.1

Remember:	12 inches = 1 foot	8 pints = 1 gallon	16 ounces = 1 pound
	3 feet = 1 yard		14 pounds = 1 stone
	1760 yards = 1 mile		2240 pounds = 1 ton

1 Copy and complete the following:

   a 2·6 m = ☐ cm   **b** 3·82 m = ☐ cm   **c** 470 cm = ☐ m

   d 90 mm = ☐ cm   **e** 4 mm = ☐ cm   **f** 1500 m = ☐ km

   g 3·5 kg = ☐ g   **h** 600 g = ☐ kg   **i** 0·28 kg = ☐ g

   j 1·9 tonnes = ☐ kg   **k** 620 ml = ☐ litre   **l** 1937 litres = ☐ ml

   m 8·2 litres = ☐ ml   **n** 3·26 litres = ☐ ml   **o** 43 g = ☐ kg

2 A shop uses 40 g of cheese in one sandwich. How many sandwiches
will the shop make if it has 3·2 kg of cheese?

3 Write the following amounts in order of size, starting with the smallest.
  a 8 cm,   0·81 m,   7·4 cm,   83 mm
  b 780 g,   0·7 kg,   738 g,   0·79 kg
  c 5 km,   57 m,   509 m,   0·6 km,   4·7 km
  d 274 ml,   0·28 litres,   0·279 litres,   275 ml,   2·14 litres

4 Which imperial unit would you use to measure:
  a the mass of a man   **b** the length of a book   **c** the height of a house

5 Mary is 4 feet 10 inches tall when she is 11 years old. Over the next 5 years she grows 7 inches. How tall is she now?

6 Jade runs 1285 yards. How much further must she run to complete 1 mile?

7 Copy and complete the following:
  a 2·5 gallons = ☐ pints   **b** 3 stone 2 pounds = ☐ pounds
  c 5 stone 9 pounds = ☐ pounds   **d** 3 miles = ☐ yards
  e 36 pints = ☐ gallons   **f** 98 pounds = ☐ stone
  g 5 tons = ☐ pounds   **h** 7 stone 12 pounds = ☐ pounds
  i $1\frac{1}{2}$ tons = ☐ pounds   **j** 5 feet 10 inches = ☐ inches

TASK M10.2

Remember: 1 inch ≈ 2·5 cm   1 ounce ≈ 30 g   1 litre ≈ 1·8 pints
            1 foot ≈ 30 cm   1 kg ≈ 2·2 pounds   1 gallon ≈ 4·5 litres
            1 yard ≈ 90 cm
            1 mile ≈ 1·6 km

1 Copy and complete:
  a 10 gallons ≈ ☐ litres   **b** 20 kg ≈ ☐ pounds
  c 4 gallons ≈ ☐ litres   **d** 6 inches ≈ ☐ cm
  e 10 miles ≈ ☐ km   **f** $2\frac{1}{2}$ feet ≈ ☐ cm
  g 180 ounces ≈ ☐ g   **h** 27 litres ≈ ☐ gallons
  i 17·5 cm ≈ ☐ inches   **j** $3\frac{1}{2}$ yards ≈ ☐ cm

2 Harry cycles 20 miles. Louise cycles 30 km. Who cycles further?

3 Tom needs 6·5 pounds of flour. If he buys a 2 kg bag of flour and a 1 kg bag of flour, will he have enough flour?

4 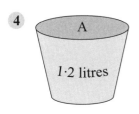 If each container is filled up with water, which container will hold the most?

5 Which amount is the smaller?
- **a** 3 gallons or 14 litres?
- **b** 8 miles or 12 km?
- **c** 5 km or 3 miles?
- **d** 5 kg or 10 pounds?
- **e** 8 yards or 700 cm?
- **f** 35 litres or 8 gallons?
- **g** 9 inches or 23 cm?
- **h** 4 feet or 1 m?

TASK M10.3

Use $\dfrac{D}{S\,T}$ to help you work out the Questions below.

1 A train travels 504 km in 4 hours. What was the average speed of the train?

2 A coach covers a distance of $225\frac{1}{2}$ km at an average speed of 73 km/hr. How long was the coach travelling for?

3 Jack cycles 3 km in 15 minutes. What was his average speed in km/hr?

4 Brenda drives from Nottingham to Leeds at an average speed of 84 km/hr. The journey takes 1 hour 30 minutes. How far is it from Nottingham to Leeds?

5 A train travels 47 km in 20 minutes. What is the speed of the train in km/hr?

6 Ellen drives 24 km from her home to work. She travels at an average speed of 32 km/hr. If she leaves home at 8:05 a.m., when will she arrive at work?

7 Distance from Leeds (miles)

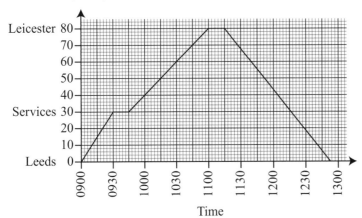

The graph at the bottom of the last page shows a car journey from Leeds to Leicester and back.

a How far from Leeds is the car at 1015?

b How far from Leeds is the car at 1036?

c Find the speed of the car between the Services and Leicester.

d On the return journey, at what time was the car 70 miles from Leeds?

e For how long did the car stop in Leicester?

f Find the speed of the car on the return journey from Leicester to Leeds.

8 Terry is travelling at 13 km/hr. Joel is moving at 3·5 m/s. Who is travelling faster?

9 A train travels 253 km at an average speed of 92 km/hr then 45 km at an average speed of 10 m/s. Find the average speed for the whole journey in km/hr.

10 Arlene travels for 48 minutes at 75 km/hr then for 1 hour 12 minutes at x km/hr. If she travels a total distance of 126 km, find the value of x.

TASK M10.4

Use $\frac{M}{D|V}$ to help you work out the Questions below.

1 A solid weighs 450 g and has a volume of 50 cm³. Find the density of this solid.

2 A liquid has a density of 2 g/cm². How much does the liquid weigh if its volume is 240 cm³?

3 A metal bar has a density of 12 g/cm³ and a mass of 360 g. Find the volume of the metal bar.

4 Copy and complete this table.

Density (g/cm³)	Mass (g)	Volume (cm³)
7		90
	240	60
8	152	
	42	0·5
13	585	
1·5		140

5 Gold has a density of 19·3 g/cm³. A gold ring has a volume of 1·1 cm³. Find the mass of the gold ring.

6 A brass handle has a volume of 17 cm³ and a mass of 139·4 g. Find the density of the brass.

7 Which has a greater volume — 102·6 g of lead with density 11·4 g/cm^3 or 78·85 g of steel with density 8·3 g/cm^3? Write down by how much.

8 The density of this metal bar is 7·4 g/cm^3.
Find the mass of this metal bar. Give your answer in kg.
(Note the length is given in metres)

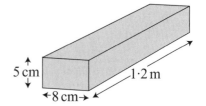

5 cm   8 cm   1·2 m

9 A metal cube of length 0·2 m has a density of 8·3 g/cm^3. A hole is bored through the cube with 485 cm^3 of metal being removed. What is the mass in kg of the remaining piece of metal?

10 A metal bar has 3 holes cut completely through its length. The cross-sectional area of each hole is y cm^2. The density of the metal is 9 g/cm^3.
Find the mass of the remaining piece of metal, giving your answer in terms of x and y.

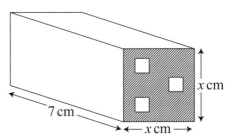

7 cm x cm x cm

TASK M10.5

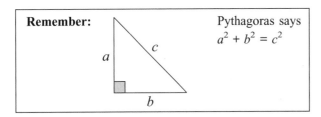

Remember:

Pythagoras says
$a^2 + b^2 = c^2$

You will need a calculator. Give your answers correct to 2 decimal places where necessary. The units are cm.

1 Find the length AB.

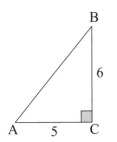

B

6

A   5   C

2 Find the length KL.

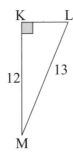

K   L

12   13

M

3 Find the length *x*.

a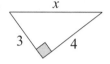

b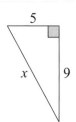

c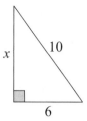

d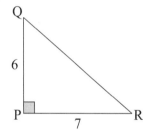

e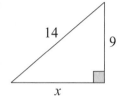

f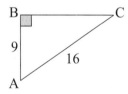

4 Find the length QR.

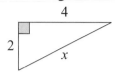

5 Find the length BC.

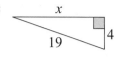

TASK M10.6

You may use a calculator. Give answers to 2 decimal places.

1 A rectangle has length 9 cm and width 7 cm. Calculate the length of its diagonal.

2 Calculate the perimeter of this triangle.

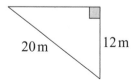

3 A ladder of length 7·5 m reaches 5·5 m up a vertical wall. How far is the foot of the ladder from the wall?

4 A plane flies 100 km due south and then a further 150 km due east. How far is the plane from its starting point?

5 Calculate the area of this triangle.

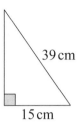

39 cm

15 cm

6 A knight on a chessboard moves 2 cm to the right then 4 cm forwards. If the knight moved *directly* from its old position to its new position, how far would it move?

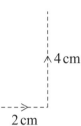

4 cm

2 cm

7 Find *x*.

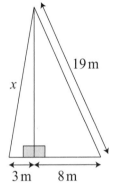

19 m

x

3 m   8 m

8 Calculate the length of the line joining $(1, 3)$ to $(5, 6)$.

9 Calculate the length of the line joining $(-2, -5)$ to $(3, 7)$.

10 Find the height of each isosceles triangle below:

a

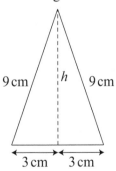

9 cm   *h*   9 cm

3 cm   3 cm

b

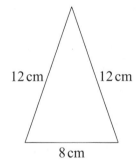

12 cm   12 cm

8 cm

11 Find the area of this isosceles triangle.

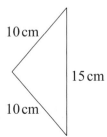

10 cm

15 cm

10 cm

12 Find the perimeter of this trapezium.

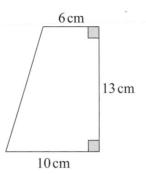

6 cm

13 cm

10 cm

TASK M10.7

In each triangle below, note the angle given and state whether the identified side is in the correct position or not.

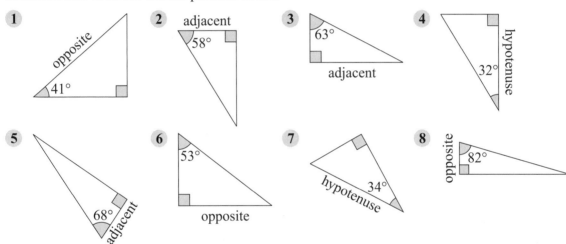

1 opposite 41°

2 adjacent 58°

3 63° adjacent

4 hypotenuse 32°

5 68° adjacent

6 53° opposite

7 hypotenuse 34°

8 opposite 82°

TASK M10.8

For each triangle below, find the sides marked with letters, correct to 3 significant figures. All lengths are in cm.

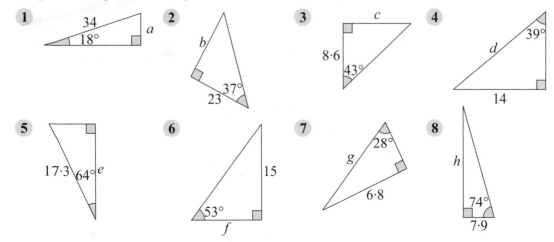

1 34 18° a

2 b 37° 23

3 c 8·6 43°

4 39° d 14

5 17·3 64° e

6 15 53° f

7 g 28° 6·8

8 h 74° 7·9

9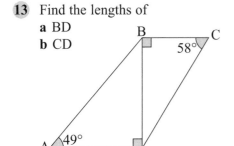

10

11

12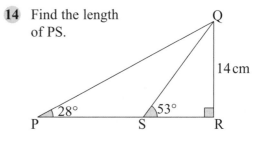

13 Find the lengths of
 a BD
 b CD

14 Find the length
 of PS.

15 Find the length of KN.

16 Find the length of TU.

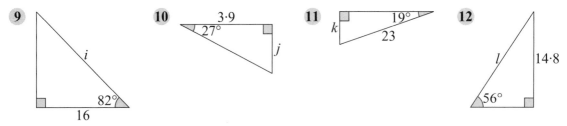

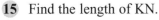

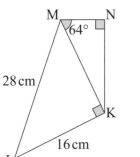

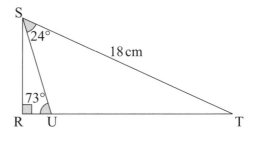

TASK M10.9

For each triangle below, find the angles marked, correct to one decimal place.
All lengths are in cm.

1 **2** **3** **4**

5 **6** **7** **8**

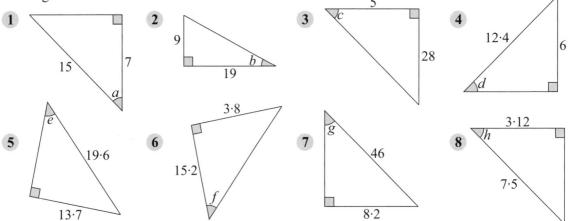

9 Find ∠RSP.

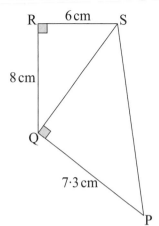

10 Find ∠ADB.

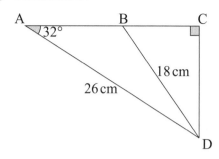

11 Find ∠ABC.

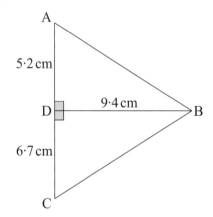

12 If PS : SR = 2 : 5, find ∠SQR.

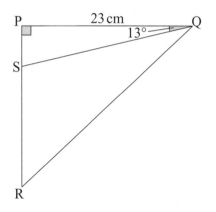

TASK M10.10

In this Exercise give each answer to 3 significant figures or 1 decimal place for angles.

1 Find ∠ABC.

2 Find PR.

3 Find LM.

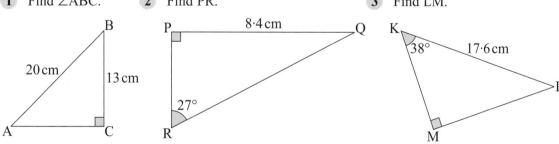

4 A builder wants a metal support to be inclined at an angle of 40° to the horizontal. If the vertical height from the bottom to the top of the support is 3·8 m, what is the length of the metal support?

5 Find the length of PQ.

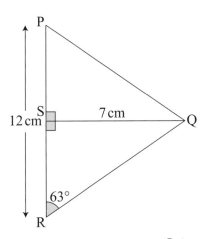

6 A wire is fixed to the ground and attached to the top of a pole of height 9 m. If the wire on the ground is 15 m from the foot of the pole, at what angle to the horizontal is the wire?

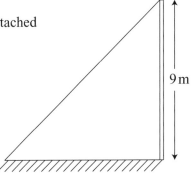

7 AC = BC
Find the area of triangle ABC.

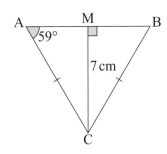

8 O is the centre of a circle of radius 6 cm. If ∠AOB = 50°, find the area of triangle AOB.

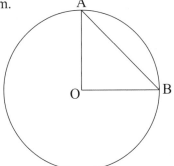

9 PQRS is a kite.
Find the length of PS.

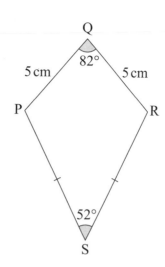

10 Find the length of AD.

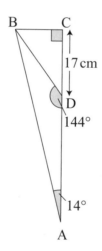

11 *Do not use a calculator in this Question.*
O is the centre of the circle.
AC is a tangent to the circle.

$\cos \angle OAB = \dfrac{12}{13}$

$\sin \angle OAB = \dfrac{5}{13}$

$\tan \angle OAB = \dfrac{5}{12}$

Find the length of AD.

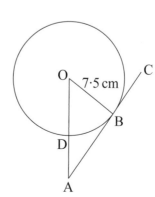

TASK E10.1

1 Write each vector as a column vector, eg. $\overrightarrow{CD} = \begin{pmatrix} 1 \\ -1 \end{pmatrix}$

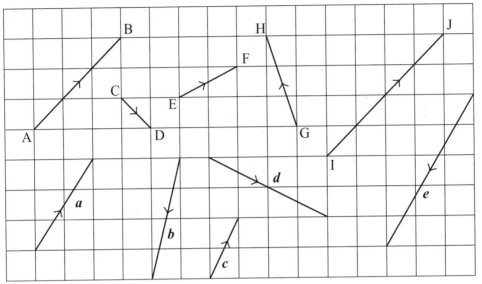

2 Calculate the length (modulus) of *a*, *b*, *c*, *d*, and *e* in Question **1**, leaving your answers in surd form.

3 Draw and label each vector below on squared paper.

$$f = \begin{pmatrix} 4 \\ -1 \end{pmatrix} \quad g = \begin{pmatrix} 2 \\ 2 \end{pmatrix} \quad h = \begin{pmatrix} -3 \\ -2 \end{pmatrix} \quad \overrightarrow{PQ} = \begin{pmatrix} -2 \\ 0 \end{pmatrix} \quad \overrightarrow{XY} = \begin{pmatrix} -5 \\ 2 \end{pmatrix}$$

4 Write down the modulus (in surd form) of the vector with the longest length in Question **3**.

TASK E10.2

1 If $k = \begin{pmatrix} 2 \\ 4 \end{pmatrix}$, $m = \begin{pmatrix} -3 \\ 2 \end{pmatrix}$ and $n = \begin{pmatrix} -5 \\ -1 \end{pmatrix}$, find as a column vector:

a $3m$ b $4n$ c $m + k$ d $2m + n$

e $5k - n$ f $2k + 3m + 2n$ g $4(m - n)$ h $\frac{1}{2}(k + 2n)$

2 Simplify the following vectors:

a $m + 2n - n$ b $2m + 3(m + 2n)$ c $\frac{1}{2}(m - n) + n$

d $p + \frac{3}{2}(q - 2p)$ e $a + \frac{2}{3}(2a - b) + \frac{1}{2}b$ f $3a - \frac{1}{2}(a + c) + 2b$

3 Make a copy of this grid then write on the letters A to H so that:

a $\overrightarrow{OA} = 2a$ b $\overrightarrow{OB} = a + 2b$

c $\overrightarrow{OC} = -b$ d $\overrightarrow{OD} = 2a - 2b$

e $\overrightarrow{OE} = -2a + b$ f $\overrightarrow{OF} = -a - b$

g $\overrightarrow{OG} = -2a - 2b$ h $\overrightarrow{OH} = 2a + 3b$

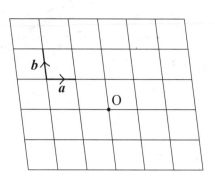

4 Express each vector in terms of a, b or c.

a $\overrightarrow{AC}$ b $\overrightarrow{CA}$ c $\overrightarrow{AD}$ d $\overrightarrow{BD}$

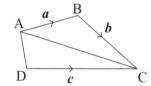

5 $\overrightarrow{KL} = \begin{pmatrix} 2 \\ 5 \end{pmatrix}$ and $\overrightarrow{MN} = \begin{pmatrix} 8 \\ 20 \end{pmatrix}$

KL is parallel to MN. *Explain* why.

6 KLMN is a rhombus.
Express each vector in terms of m and n.

a $\overrightarrow{KN}$ b $\overrightarrow{MN}$ c $\overrightarrow{LN}$ d $\overrightarrow{MK}$

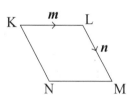

7 M has co-ordinates $(3, 1)$.

$\overrightarrow{MN} = \begin{pmatrix} 4 \\ 2 \end{pmatrix}$ and $\overrightarrow{MP} = \begin{pmatrix} 3 \\ -1 \end{pmatrix}$.

a Find the co-ordinates of N.
b Find the co-ordinates of P.
c Find $\overrightarrow{NP}$ as a column vector.

TASK E10.3

1 $\overrightarrow{ML} = p$ and $\overrightarrow{LN} = q$.
S is the midpoint of ML and T cuts MN in the ratio $2 : 1$.
Express the following vectors in terms of p and q.

a $\overrightarrow{MS}$ b $\overrightarrow{MN}$ c $\overrightarrow{MT}$

d $\overrightarrow{ST}$ e $\overrightarrow{SN}$ f $\overrightarrow{TL}$

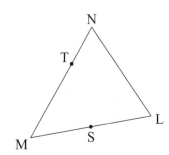

2 $\overrightarrow{OA} = 2\overrightarrow{OM}$; $\overrightarrow{OC} = 4\overrightarrow{ON}$

Express the following vectors in terms of *a* and *b*.

a $\overrightarrow{AB}$ b $\overrightarrow{AC}$

c *Explain* why A, B and C are collinear
(lie on the same straight line)

d Find the ratio AB : AC.

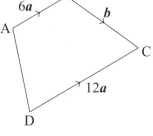

3 X cuts AB in the ratio 2 : 1.
Y cuts DC in the ratio 1 : 2.
Express the following vectors in terms of *a* and *b*.

a $\overrightarrow{XY}$ b $\overrightarrow{AD}$

c *Explain* why AXYD is a parallelogram.

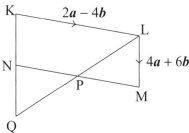

4 KLMN is a parallelogram.
P is the midpoint of MN.
$\overrightarrow{PQ} = a + 5b$

Express the following vectors in terms of *a* and *b*.

a $\overrightarrow{KN}$ b $\overrightarrow{LP}$ c $\overrightarrow{LQ}$ d $\overrightarrow{KQ}$

e *Explain* why K, N and Q are collinear
(lie on the same straight line)

f Find the ratio KN : KQ.

DATA 2   11

TASK M11.1

Give answers to one decimal place when appropriate.

1 When they last recycled something, 600 children were asked if they recycled
paper, bottles or cans. The information is shown in the two-way table below.

	paper	bottles	cans	Total
Boys		73	89	
Girls				352
Total	306	131		600

a Copy and complete the two-way table.

b How many girls recycled paper last time they recycled something?

c What percentage of the children recycled cans?

2 Some people were asked if they would rather watch a film on a dvd, at the cinema or go to the theatre.
The results are shown below: M = Male, F = Female
d = dvd, c = cinema, t = theatre

M, c   M, c   F, c   F, d   F, c
F, d   F, t   F, d   M, t   M, c
M, c   F, c   M, c   F, t   F, d
F, d   F, d   M, t   M, d   F, c

a Put these results into a two-way table.
b What percentage of the males chose the theatre?

3 500 students in the Kingsley High School were asked what they planned to do after Year 11. The results are shown in the two-way table below.

	stay in 6th. form	go to college	leave education	Total
Year 10			26	
Year 11	120	109	31	
Total	206			500

a Copy and complete the two-way table.
b One of these students is picked at random. Write down the *probability* that the student is in Year 10.
c One of these students is picked at random. Write down the *probability* that the student plans to go to College.

4 1000 people in Birmingham were asked how they travel to work. The information is shown in the two-way table below.

	car	walk	bike	train	Total
Birmingham	314	117		69	
Nottingham		175	41		
Total	530		72		1000

a Copy and complete the two-way table.
b One of the people from Birmingham *only* is chosen. What is the probability that this person travels to work by bike?
c What percentage of the people asked travel to work by train?

TASK M11.2

In Questions **1** and **2**, work out the angle for each item and draw a pie chart.

1 Favourite type of film

film	frequency
adventure	6
comedy	18
horror	7
romance	2
cartoon	12

2 Favourite colour

colour	frequency
blue	23
green	8
red	28
yellow	41
purple	4
other	16

3 300 people were asked what their favourite hot drink is. The pie chart shows the findings. How many people chose:
a coffee **b** others **c** tea

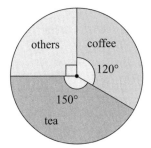

4 This pie chart shows the favourite 'spirits' chosen by 480 people. How many people chose:
a vodka **b** gin **c** brandy

5 10,000 people were surveyed about which continent they would prefer to buy their car from. The pie chart shows this information. Find the angle on the pie chart for:
a Europe **b** Asia **c** America

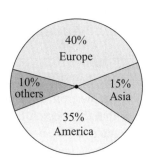

6 The pie charts below show the favourite sports of students from Canning High School and Henton Park School.

Canning High School

Henton Park School

Explain why you *cannot* say that more students like football in Canning High School than in Henton Park School.

TASK M11.3

1 Write down what X and Y might be to give this scatter graph.

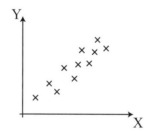

2 The table below shows the heights and neck lengths of 14 people.

height (cm)	177	187	195	162	200	175	192	186	165	200	172	198	181	190
neck length (cm)	6·9	7·5	7·5	5·5	8·5	6·1	6·8	6·8	6	8	5·7	7·7	6·9	7·8

a Copy and complete this scatter graph to show the data in the table.
b Describe the correlation.
c Draw the line of best fit.
d A person is 184 cm tall. Use your line of best fit to find out the person's likely neck length.
e Another person has a neck length of 7·7 cm. How tall is that person likely to be?

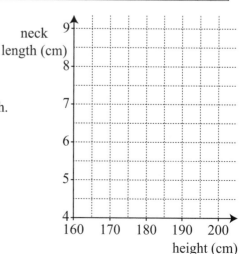

3 This scatter graph shows information about cars.
Write down what you think Y might be.

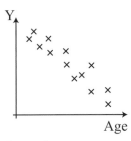

4 A golfer records his weekly average score and how many hours be
practises each week (in golf a score of 70 is *better* than a score of 80!).
The information is shown in the table below.

Weekly average score	79	75	87	81	84	73	77	88	72	78	84	76
Weekly hours practising	22	24	19	21	22	23	24	17	26	22	19	21

a Draw a scatter graph to show this data.
Use the *x*-axis for the weekly average
score from 70 to 90. Use the *y*-axis for
the weekly hours practising from 0 to 30.
b Describe the correlation in this
scatter graph.
c Draw the line of best fit.
d If the golfer practised for 25 hours
one week, what average score would
you expect the golfer to get that week?

TASK M11.4

1 A local post office sells cards. The table below shows how many cards
were sold during a one-year period.

month	Jan	Feb	Mar	Apr	May	Jun	Jul	Aug	Sep	Oct	Nov	Dec
number of cards	60	440	80	380	100	40	60	20	300	460	580	560

a Draw a line graph for the information in this table.
b Find the mean average for the first 4 months: Jan, Feb, Mar, Apr.
Plot this average on the graph at the midpoint of the 4 months.
c Keep moving along one month and finding the 4-point moving
average (ie. use a group of 4 months). Plot the new moving average
on the graph each time.
d Join up the moving average points with a dotted line. Comment on
the trend of card sales during this year. Write down any reasons for
this trend.

2 The table below shows how many houses have been sold by an estate agent during a 15-year period.

year	1991	1992	1993	1994	1995	1996	1997	1998	1999	2000	2001	2002	2003	2004	2005
number of houses sold	135	45	135	150	30	180	165	60	180	135	165	195	45	180	150

    a Draw a line graph for the information in this table.
    b Find the 3-point moving average (ie. use groups of 3 years). Plot the new moving average on the graph each time.
    c Join up the moving average points with a dotted line. Comment on the trend of house sales during these 15 years.

3 The table below shows how many people visit a local castle each day during a 3-week period.

	Mon	Tue	Wed	Thu	Fri	Sat	Sun
week 1	90	75	100	115	140	210	180
week 2	55	75	114	115	147	224	187
week 3	62	68	107	129	182	210	201

    a Draw a line graph for the information in this table.
    b Find the 7-point moving average.
    c Plot the moving average points on the graph and join them up with a dotted line.
    d Comment on the trend shown.

TASK E11.1

1 Write down which samples below are likely to be representative.
For any sample which is not representative give a reason why it is not.
    a To find out the average number of cars owned by each family in a particular city.
The sample is chosen by randomly selecting 10% of the streets in the city and visiting each house to establish the number of cars.
    b To find out who people will vote for at the next Local Election in a certain town.
The sample is chosen by asking people as they enter the town's largest supermarket.
    c To find out the percentage of the crowd entering a football ground who are female.
The sample is chosen by recording the sex of every 10th. person as they pass through the gates.
    d To find out the average amount of time people spend exercising each week.
The sample is chosen by asking people as they enter a local Gym.

e   To find out the average number of computers per household.
    The sample is chosen by selecting at random people from 10% of
    the addresses from the electoral register.
f   To find out the number of birds which visit gardens in the UK.
    The sample is chosen by selecting every 20th. name from every telephone
    directory in the UK and asking each of these people to record the number of birds.

2   Describe how you would select a representative sample for each of the following:
a   To find out the most popular rock bands of people under 18 years old.
b   To find out the most popular holiday destinations of people in Scotland.
c   To survey pupils in a school about how they get to and from school each day.
d   To investigate the most popular drinks of people in a certain city.

TASK E11.2

1   625 people go to the theatre to watch a famous comedian. 392 of these
people are male. A stratified sample of 50 people is to be taken from
the males and females in the audience to find out their opinions on the
concert. How many males and how many females will be chosen?

2   900 people return from their holidays. 284 people went skiing, 109
visited Australasia, 321 took city breaks in Europe and the rest had
visited the Caribbean.
A holiday company wishes to find out about the quality of service in the
hotels these people stayed in. They decide to take a stratified sample of
70 people. What should be the sample size for each of the holiday
destinations: skiing, Australasia, European cities and the Caribbean?

3   Rachel needs to survey opinions from people visiting the local
swimming pool. Explain how Rachel could take a simple random sample.

4   The table below shows the number of people who voted for each party
at a General Election in one constituency.

Party	Number of votes
Labour	16 201
Conservative	12 374
Liberal Democrat	9 812
Green	7 104
Others	387

It is wanted to take a stratified sample of 2000 people to find out more
about their opinions on major issues.
How many people from each chosen Party would be selected in the
stratified sample?

5 In a certain school, a choice from 3 languages is offered in Year 7.
The take-up is shown below.

Language	Number of pupils
French	139
German	69
Spanish	42

A sample of 25 pupils is to be taken to question them about their attitudes to languages.
a Explain why you would want to use a stratified sample.
b Work out how many pupils you would want in your sample from each Language.

ALGEBRA 3   12

TASK M12.1

1 **a** Draw these axes.
   b If $3x + y = 6$, find the value of y when $x = 0$.
   c If $3x + y = 6$, find the value of x when $y = 0$.
   d Plot 2 points from **b** and **c** and join them up to make the straight line $3x + y = 6$.

2 Draw each line below with the 'cover-up' method.
You need to find the 2 points first then draw the axes big enough.
   a $2x + 3y = 12$ **b** $3x + 7y = 21$
   c $8x + 5y = 40$ **d** $4x - 3y = 24$

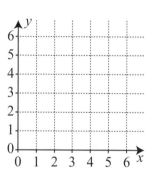

TASK M12.2

1 Use the graph to solve the simultaneous equations below:
   a $x + y = 6$ **b** $x - 2y = -6$
       $2x - y = 6$ $2x - y = 6$

   c $x + y = 6$
       $x - 2y = -6$

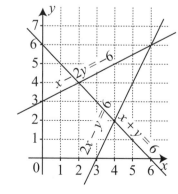

2 **a** Draw an x-axis from 0 to 7.
Draw a y-axis from -5 to 5.
b Use the cover-up method to draw the line $2x + 3y = 12$.
c Use the cover-up method to draw the line $4x - 2y = 8$.
d Use your graph to solve the simultaneous equations $2x + 3y = 12$
$$4x - 2y = 8$$

3 By drawing graphs, solve the following pairs of simultaneous equations:

a $x + y = 4$
$y = x + 2$

b $5x + 2y = 20$
$x - 2y = -8$

c $2x + y = 7$
$y = 2x - 5$

TASK M12.3

1 Add together the simultaneous equations $3x + 2y = 7$
and $7x - 2y = 3$
Use your answer to find the value of x.
Use this value of x to find the value of y.

Solve the simultaneous equations

2 $2x + 3y = 12$
$5x + 3y = 21$

3 $4x + y = 13$
$4x + 3y = 23$

4 $3x + y = 16$
$2x - y = 9$

5 $4x - 3y = 0$
$7x + 3y = 33$

6 $5x + 4y = 24$
$3x - 4y = -24$

7 $2x - 5y = -12$
$3x - 5y = -13$

8 $4x + 2y = 10$
$7x - 2y = 34$

9 $3x + 5y = -11$
$3x - 4y = -2$

10 $2x - 2y = -16$
$3x - 2y = -21$

TASK M12.4

Solve the simultaneous equations

1 $3x + 4y = 17$
$6x + y = 20$

2 $2a + 3b = 14$
$3a + 2b = 11$

3 $4m + 3n = 26$
$3m - 5n = -24$

4 $5c - 4d = 21$
$2c - 3d = 7$

5 $2p - 3q = -11$
$p + 4q = 11$

6 $7a + 3b = 22$
$5a - 2b = 24$

7 $3m + 4n = 11$
$2m + 6n = 9$

8 $4x - 3y = 2$
$5x + 7y = -19$

9 $10x - 3y = -14$
$4x - 5y = -17$

10 $3p - 2q + 18 = 0$
$5p + 7q = 32$

11 $8c + 3d = -35$
$5c = -22 - 2d$

12 $6x - 8y = 1$
$4x + 12y - 5 = 0$

TASK M12.5

Answer these Questions by forming a pair of simultaneous equations then solving them.

1. Darren buys 3 pairs of socks and 2 pairs of underpants for £25. Colin buys 2 pairs of socks and 7 pairs of underpants for £62. What is the cost of a pair of socks and a pair of underpants?

2. The sum of two numbers is 19. The difference between four times one number and the other number is 41. Find the values of the two numbers.

3. Howlton primary school buy 10 solar calculators and 30 battery calculators for £210. Merryfield primary school buy 15 solar calculators and 8 battery calculators for £130. Find the cost of one solar calculator and one battery calculator.

4. Penny buys 5 adult tickets and 3 child tickets for the theatre. The tickets cost her a total of £164. Barney buys 4 adult tickets and 4 child tickets at a total cost of £152. Find the cost of one adult ticket and one child ticket.

5. A straight line passes through the points $(2, 11)$ and $(-1, 2)$. The equation of a straight line is $y = mx + c$. Find the values of m and c.

6. A bookstall is selling all its hard backs at the same price and all its paper backs at the same price. A woman buys 7 hard backs and 5 paper backs for £61·40. A man buys 11 hard backs and 7 paper backs for £93·10. Find the price of one hard back and one paper back.

7. A pub offers a special discount for senior citizens. A set meal is normally £11 but the price for a senior citizen is £8. One day the pub sells three times as many senior citizen set meals as normal priced set meals and takes £420. How many senior citizen meals and normal priced meals did the pub sell on that day?

8. Charlie has four times as many sweets as Anna. Charlie eats 14 sweets and Anna eats 2 sweets. If Charlie now has three times as many sweets as Anna, how many sweets have Charlie and Anna each got *now*?

TASK M12.6

In Questions 1 to 6, write down the next 2 numbers. What is the rule for each sequence?

1. 40, 20, 10, 5, ...
2. 4·9, 4·1, 3·3, 2·5, ...
3. $\frac{1}{2}$, $1\frac{1}{4}$, 2, $2\frac{3}{4}$, ...
4. 4, 12, 36, 108, ...
5. 3000, 300, 30, 3, ...
6. $-1, -2, -4, -8, ...$

7. The first four terms of a sequence are 2, 8, 14, 20. The 50th term in the sequence is 296. Write down the 49th term.

8 How many small squares are needed for
   a shape 5
   b shape 6

shape 1   shape 2   shape 3   shape 4

In Questions **9** to **12** find the next *2 numbers* in each sequence
(it may help you to work out the 2$^{nd.}$ differences).

9 2, 5, 10, 17, . . .

10 0, 3, 8, 15, . . .

11 2, 6, 12, 20, . . .

12 2, 8, 16, 26, . . .

13 The first five terms of a sequence are 1, 2, 4, 8, 16, . . .
   The 9$^{th.}$ term in the sequence is 512.
   Write down the 10$^{th.}$ term of the sequence.

14 Find the next 2 numbers in the sequence below. Try to explain
   the pattern.
   0, 1, 3, 7, 15, . . .

15 Match each $n^{th.}$ term formula below to its corresponding sequence:
   a 1, 6, 11, 16, . . .
   b 2, 5, 10, 17, . . .
   c 5, 7, 9, 11, . . .
   d 2, 6, 12, 20, . . .
   e 3, 9, 27, 81, . . .
   f 4, 8, 12, 16, . . .

   A $2n + 3$ B $n^2 + 1$

   C $4n$ D 3^n

   E $n(n + 1)$ F $5n - 4$

TASK M12.7

1 Match up each sequence to the correct $n^{th.}$ term formula.

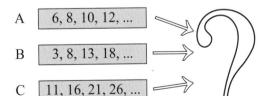

   A 6, 8, 10, 12, ...
   B 3, 8, 13, 18, ...
   C 11, 16, 21, 26, ...
   D 8, 10, 12, 14, ...

   P $n^{th.}$ term $= 2n + 6$
   Q $n^{th.}$ term $= 5n - 2$
   R $n^{th.}$ term $= 2n + 4$
   S $n^{th.}$ term $= 5n + 6$

2 Find the $n^{th.}$ term of each sequence below:

    a 7, 10, 13, 16, ...   **b** 9, 16, 23, 30, ...

    c 1, 10, 19, 28, ...   **d** 6, 14, 22, 30, ...

    e 30, 26, 22, 18, ...   **f** 18, 13, 8, 3, ...

    g 8, 12, 16, 20, ...   **h** 22, 19, 16, 13, ...

3

    $n = 1$ $n = 2$ $n = 3$

    $s = 8$ $s = 15$ $s =$

    a Draw the next shape in the sequence.

    b Let n = shape number and s = number of sticks. Complete a table of values for n and s.

    c Use the table and $1^{st.}$ difference to find a formula for the number of sticks (s) for the shape number n.

        Use values of n to check if each formula is correct.

    d Use the formula to find out how many sticks are in shape number 40.

4 Repeat Question **3** for the sequence below:

  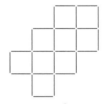

    $n = 1$ $n = 2$ $n = 3$

5 Matthew decides to save money in the following way:

    He saves £1 in the first week, £1·20 in the second week, £1·40 in the third week, and so on.

    a How much would he save in the $n^{th.}$ week?

    b How much would he save in the $8^{th.}$ week?

    c In which week would he first save at least £5?

    d After 10 weeks, Matthew wants to buy a tennis racquet which costs £19·99. He realises that he hasn't saved quite enough, but by how much is he short?

6 A series of rows of tins are piled on top of one another. The bottom row has 35 tins and each row has two fewer tins than the row below it.

    a How many tins are there in the $n^{th.}$ row from the bottom?

    b What is the maximum number of rows of tins?

TASK E12.1

1 The nth term of a sequence is given by $n^2 - n$.
 a Write down the 1st term of the sequence.
 b Write down the 4th term of the sequence.
 c Write down the 10th term of the sequence.

2 Find the nth term of each sequence below:
 a 5, 8, 13, 20, 29, ...   **b** −1, 2, 7, 14, 23, ...
 c 0, 2, 6, 12, 20, ...   **d** 6, 14, 24, 36, 50, ...

3 Here is a sequence of rectangles made from squares.
 Let n = shape number and s = number of squares

 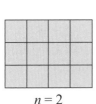 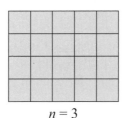 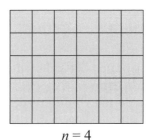

    $n = 1$ $n = 2$ $n = 3$ $n = 4$

 a Find a formula for s in terms of n.
 b How many squares in shape number 25?

4 Find **i** the nth term and **ii** the 20th term of each sequence below:
 a 3, 12, 27, 48, 75   **b** 5, 11, 21, 35, 53
 c 7, 18, 33, 52, 75   **d** 5, 18, 37, 62, 93

5 Consider the sequence: −3   −4   −3   0   5
 a Find the nth term.
 b Find the value of n for which the nth term = 140.

TASK E12.2

1 $(x + 3)^2 = (x + 3)(x + 3) = x^2 + 6x + 9$
 Express $x^2 + 6x + 13$ in the form $(x + a)^2 + b$, giving the values of a and b.

2 $(x - 5)^2 = (x - 5)(x - 5) = x^2 - 10x + 25$
 Express $x^2 - 10x + 18$ in the form $(x + c)^2 + d$, giving the values of c and d.

3 Write the following in the form $(x + a)^2 + b$ where a and b are numbers to be determined:
 a $x^2 + 16x + 30$ **b** $x^2 - 4x + 1$ **c** $x^2 - 3x + 2$

4 Copy and complete:
$$x^2 - 8x + 3 = 0$$
$$(x - 4)^2 - \square + 3 = 0$$
$$(x - 4)^2 = \square$$
$$x - 4 = \sqrt{\square} \text{ or } -\sqrt{\square}$$
$$x = 4 + \sqrt{\square} \text{ or } 4 - \sqrt{\square}$$

5 Solve the following quadratic equations by completing the square (leaving your answers in the form $a \pm \sqrt{b}$ where appropriate):

a $x^2 + 6x + 4 = 0$ **b** $x^2 - 12x + 21 = 0$
c $x^2 - 20x + 90 = 0$ **d** $x^2 + 5x + 2 = 0$

6 $3x^2 + 18x + 42 = a((x + b)^2 + c)$. Find the values of a, b and c.

7 $4x^2 - 16x + 44 = p((x - q)^2 + r)$. Find the values of p, q and r.

8 Solve $x^2 + 8x + 13 = 0$ by completing the square, giving your answer to 3 significant figures.

9 By completing the square, find the minimum y-value of the curve $y = x^2 - 4x + 7$.

10 By completing the square on the denominator, find the maximum value of the function $f(x) = \dfrac{6}{x^2 + 6x + 11}$. What value of x gives this maximum value?

TASK E12.3

Remember: if $ax^2 + bx + c = 0$ then $x = \dfrac{-b \pm \sqrt{b^2 - 4ac}}{2a}$

Use the formula to solve the following quadratic equations, giving each answer to 3 significant figures.

1 $x^2 + 9x + 4 = 0$ **2** $x^2 + 4x - 1 = 0$ **3** $x^2 - 6x - 2 = 0$

4 $x^2 + 8x + 3 = 0$ **5** $2x^2 + 3x - 7 = 0$ **6** $5x^2 + 9x + 1 = 0$

7 $2x(2x - 3) = 1$ **8** $9x^2 + 5x - 2 = 0$ **9** $3x + \dfrac{3}{x} = 7$

Use the formula to solve the following quadratic equations, leaving each answer in the form $\dfrac{p \pm \sqrt{q}}{r}$.

10 $x^2 + 5x + 3 = 0$ **11** $5x^2 - 2x - 4 = 0$ **12** $x + 7 + \dfrac{11}{x} = 0$

TASK E12.4

In this Exercise give answers to 3 significant figures when appropriate.

1 A rectangle is such that its length is 2 metres longer than its width.
   a If the width of rectangle is x metres then find expressions for the length and the area of the rectangle in terms of x.
   b If the area is 5 m^2, show that $x^2 + 2x - 5 = 0$.
   c Solve this equation to find the value of x.

2 A rectangle is 34 m longer than it is wide. If the diagonal of the rectangle is 50 m then:
   a By letting the width be x, prove that
   $$x^2 + 34x - 672 = 0$$
   b Solve this equation to find the dimensions of the rectangle.

3 A triangle whose area is 76 cm^2 is such that the base is 3 cm longer than twice the height. If the height of the triangle is h then:
   a Write down an expression for the base of the triangle in terms of h.
   b Write down a quadratic equation involving h.
   c Solve this equation to find h (you may use the fact that $19 \times 16 = 304$).

4 50 m of fencing is arranged so that it encloses a rectangular area of 154 m^2. If w is the width of the rectangle then:
   a Find the length of the rectangle in terms of w.
   b Write down a quadratic equation involving w.
   c Solve this equation to find w.

5 Two positive numbers are such that the bigger one is 3 less than twice the smaller one. Their product is 35. If the smaller of the two numbers is x then:
   a Write down an expression for the larger number in terms of x.
   b Write down a quadratic equation involving x.
   c Solve this equation to find x.

6 Two circles are cut out of a rectangular sheet of metal. The larger circle has a radius r and the smaller circle has a radius 5 cm less than the larger circle. If the shaded area is 250 cm^2, find the radius of the smaller circle.

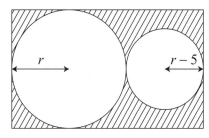

TASK E12.5

Solve the following simultaneous equations

1 $y = x^2 + 4$
    $y = 3x + 2$

2 $x^2 + y^2 = 40$
    $y = x + 4$

3 $xy = 12$
    $y = 2x - 2$

4 $x^2 + y^2 = 20$
    $y = 5x - 6$

5 Find the co-ordinates of M and N by solving
   the simultaneous equations
   $y = 7 - 3x$
   $y = 5 - x^2$

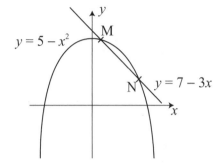

TASK E12.6

1 **a** Using a table of values, plot the graph of
      $y = 3^x$ from -3 to 3.
   b From your graph find the value of y when $x = 1.8$.
   c From your graph find the value of x when $y = 13$.

2 The population in the town of Carwick is in decline. The population, P,
   after t years is given by the formula
   $P = 2000 (0.97)^t$
   a Find the initial population P.
   b Find the population after 5 years.
   c Plot a graph showing the population over the first 10 years.
   d After how many years will the population have declined to 1600
      (give your answer to 1 decimal place)?

3 The curve $y = pq^x$ passes through (0, 4) and (2, 36).
   a Find the value of p.
   b Find the value of q (q is a positive constant).
   c Find the value of y when $x = 3$.

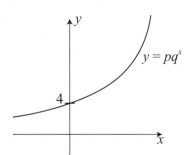

4 The curve $y = 5n^{-x} + c$ passes through $(0, 2)$ and $(1, -\frac{1}{2})$.
   a Find the value of c.
   b Find the value of n.
   c Find the value of y when $x = 2$.

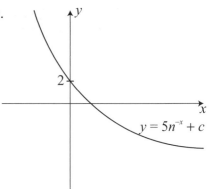

$$y = 5n^{-x} + c$$

TASK E12.7

1 Use this graph to solve (to 1 decimal place)
   a $x^2 + 5x + 1 = 0$
   b $x^2 + 5x + 1 = 2x + 4$
   c $x^2 + 3x - 3 = 0$
   d $x^2 + 5x + 2 = 0$

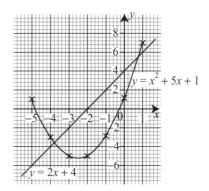

$$y = x^2 + 5x + 1$$
$$y = 2x + 4$$

2 Use this graph to solve (to 1 decimal place)
   a $x^2 - 3x - 2 = 0$
   b $x^2 - 3x - 3 = 0$
   c $x^2 - 3x + 1 = 0$
   d $x^2 - 3x - 2 = 2 - 2x$

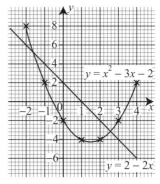

$$y = x^2 - 3x - 2$$
$$y = 2 - 2x$$

3 **a** Draw the graph of $y = x^2 - 2x$ for x-values from -2 to 4.
   b On the same axes, draw the graph of $y = x + 1$.
   c Use your graphs to solve (to 1 decimal place)
     i $x^2 - 2x = 1$
     ii $x^2 - 2x - 4 = 0$
     iii $x^2 - 2x = x + 1$
     iv $x^2 - 3x - 1 = 0$

4 If the graph of $y = x^2 + 4x - 2$ has been drawn, write down the equation of each line which should be drawn to solve each of the following equations:
   a $x^2 + 4x - 2 = 3x + 1$ **b** $x^2 + 3x - 2 = 0$ **c** $x^2 + 5x - 4 = 0$

SHAPE 4   13

TASK M13.1

Give answers to one decimal place if necessary.

Find the area of each shape below. All lengths are in cm.

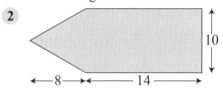 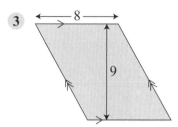

4 The area of the parallelogram is
equal to the area of the
trapezium. Find the value of *x*.

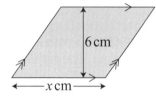
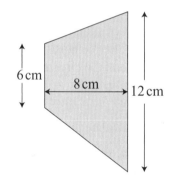

5 Find the shaded area.

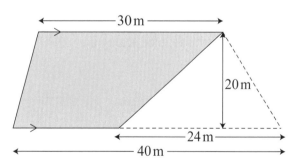

6 Find the shaded area.

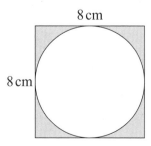

7 Find the area of each shape. All arcs are either semi-circles or quarter circles and the units are cm.

a

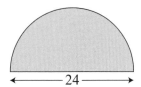

b

c

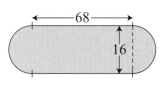

8 Find each shaded area below. All lengths are in cm.

a

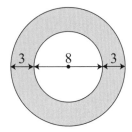

b

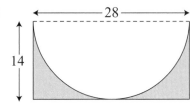

c

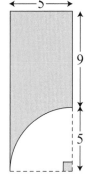

9 A circular pond has a radius of 13 m. A path goes all the way round the circumference of the pond. The path is 1·2 m wide throughout.
Find the area of the path.

10 Calculate the radius of a circle of area 68 cm².

11 The area of this parallelogram is 112·5 cm².
Calculate the value of x.

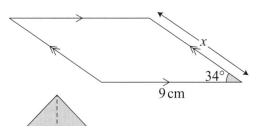

12 Find the area of this regular pentagon.

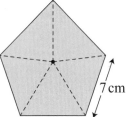

7 cm

TASK E13.1

Find the area of each triangle below, giving the answer to one decimal place.

1

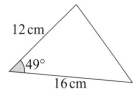

2

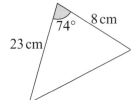

3

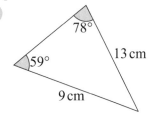

Find the value of the letter in each triangle below.

4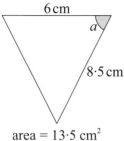
6 cm
a
8·5 cm
area = 13·5 cm²

5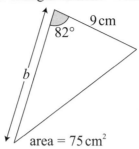
9 cm
82°
b
area = 75 cm²

6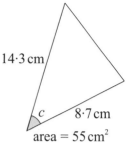
14·3 cm
c
8·7 cm
area = 55 cm²

7 area triangle ABC = 48 cm²
area triangle ABD = 120 cm²
Calculate the length of CD.

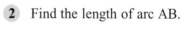

A
17 cm
23°
D   C   B

8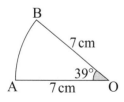
18 cm
38°
x

The area of this triangle is equal to the area of this trapezium. Calculate the value of x.

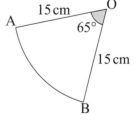
12 cm   5 cm
6 cm

TASK E13.2

In this Exercise, O is always the centre of the circle. Give answers to one decimal place.

1 Find the length of arc AB.

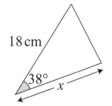
B
7 cm
39°
A   7 cm   O

2 Find the length of arc AB.

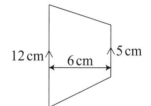
15 cm   O
A   65°
15 cm
B

3 The arc PQ = 9 cm.
Find ∠POQ.

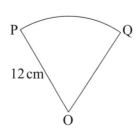
P   Q
12 cm
O

In Questions ④ to ⑥, find the perimeter of each shape, leaving answers in terms of π.

4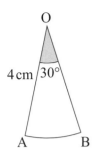

5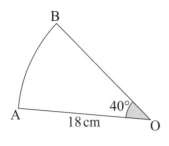

6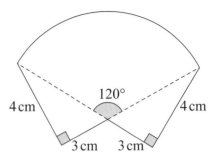

7 Use a calculator to find the perimeter of the shaded area.

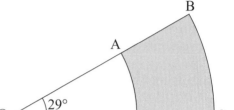

8 Use a calculator to find the perimeter of the shaded area.

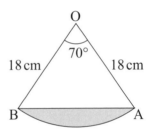

TASK E13.3

In this Exercise, O is always the centre of the circle. Give answers to one decimal place.

In Questions ① to ③, find each shaded area.

1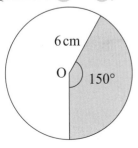

2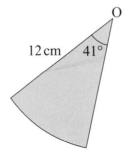

3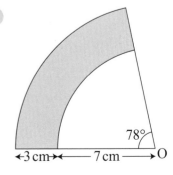

4 Show that the area of this sector is exactly $\frac{16\pi}{9}$ cm².

5 ODC is a sector of radius 4 cm.
Find the shaded area, leaving your answer in terms of π.

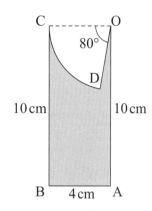

6 Find the value of θ if the area of the sector is 90 cm².

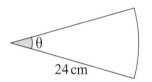

7 Find the area of the shaded segment.

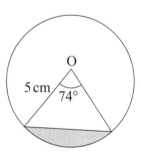

8 If AB = 13 cm, find the area of the shaded segment.

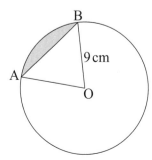

TASK M13.2

> **Remember:** 1 m³ = 1000 l = 1000 000 cm³
> 1 m² = 10 000 cm²

1 Find the volume of each prism below:

a

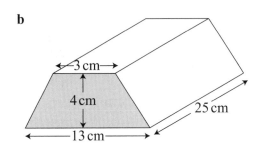

6 m
4 m
9 m
3 m
12 m

b

3 cm
4 cm
25 cm
13 cm

2 Which is the greater amount? 7·2 m³ or 7 090 000 cm³

3 True or false? 6·3 m² = 630 cm²

4 A rectangular tank has a length of 8 m and a width of 6 m. How high is the tank if it can hold 240 000 litres of water when full?

5 Copy and complete

  a 4 m³ = ☐ cm³   **b** 2·9 m³ = ☐ cm³   **c** 8 m² = ☐ cm²

  d 7·48 m² = ☐ cm²   **e** 6 000 000 cm³ = ☐ m³   **f** 6 m³ = ☐ litres

  g 6 000 000 cm² = ☐ m² **h** 5·16 m³ = ☐ litres   **i** 38 000 cm² = ☐ m²

6 Find the 'exact' volume of each prism below, leaving your answers in terms of π.

a

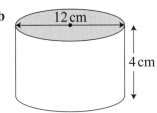

3 cm
10 cm

b

12 cm
4 cm

7 A pipe of diameter 8 cm and length 3 m is half full of water. How many litres of water are in the pipe?

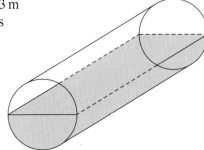

8 Find the volume of this prism.

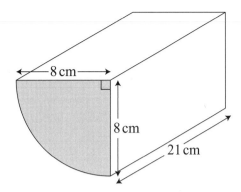

9 A cylindrical bucket has a diameter of
30 cm and a height of 35 cm.
How many full bucket loads of water
are needed to fill up the tank
opposite?

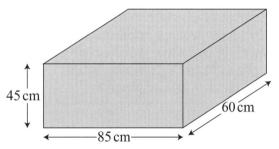

10 The height of a cylinder of capacity 3·5 litres is twice
its radius. Calculate the radius of the cylinder.

TASK E13.4

Remember:	sphere	pyramid	cone
	volume = $\frac{4}{3}\pi r^3$	volume = $\frac{1}{3} \times$ (base area) $\times h$	volume = $\frac{1}{3}\pi r^2 h$

In this Exercise give answers to 3 significant figures where necessary.

1 Find the volume of each solid.

a   **b**   **c**

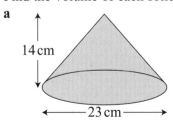

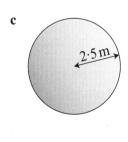

2 A hemisphere and a cone are both made from the same material. The
cone has a base diameter of 8 cm and a perpendicular height of 6 cm.
The hemisphere has a diameter of 7 cm. Which solid weighs more?

3 A sphere has a volume of 80 cm³. Find the radius of the sphere.

4 Find the 'exact' volume of each solid, leaving your answers in terms of π.

a

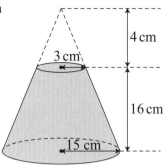

4 cm

3 cm

16 cm

15 cm

b

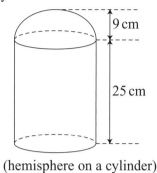

9 cm

25 cm

(hemisphere on a cylinder)

5 A bowl is in the shape of a hemisphere with diameter 18 cm. Water is poured into the bowl at a rate of 12 cm^3/s. How long will it take to fill the bowl completely?

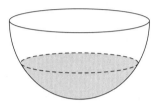

6 A pyramid has a square base of side length 8 cm and a perpendicular height of 17 cm. The pyramid has the same volume as a cone of base radius 6·5 cm. Find the perpendicular height of the cone.

7 A metal cylinder has diameter 4·8 cm and a height of 8·3 cm. 75 identical cylinders are melted down to make a single sphere. Calculate the diameter of the sphere.

TASK E13.5

> **Remember:**   sphere   cylinder   cone
> surface area = $4\pi r^2$ curved surface area = $2\pi rh$ curved surface area = πrl
>   where l is the slant height

In this Exercise give answers to 3 significant figures where necessary.

1 Find the *curved* surface area of each solid.

a

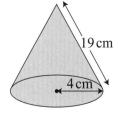

19 cm

4 cm

b

9 cm

c

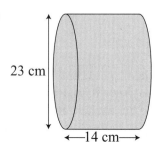

23 cm

←14 cm→

2 Find the *total* surface area of this cone, leaving your answer in terms of π.

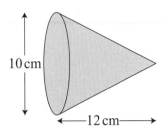

10 cm

12 cm

3 A sphere has a surface are of 480 cm². Calculate its diameter.

4 The curved surface area of a hemisphere is 72π cm². What is the *total* surface area of the hemisphere?

5 A cone is attached to a cylinder of diameter 15 cm as shown. The perpendicular heights of the cylinder and the cone are both equal to the diameter of the cylinder. Find the *total* surface area of the combined solid.

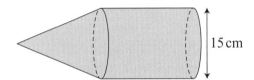

15 cm

6 A cylinder has a radius of 2 cm and a height of 10 cm. A cone has a radius of 3 cm. The total surface area of the cone is equal to the total surface area of the cylinder. Show that the perpendicular height of the cone is $4\sqrt{10}$ cm.

TASK M13.3

1 **a** *Explain* why these triangles are similar.
b Find x.

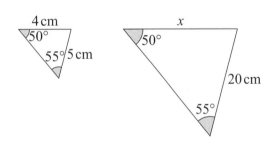

4 cm
50°
55° 5 cm

x
50°
20 cm
55°

2 Rectangles A and B are similar. Find x.

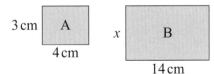

3 cm A
4 cm

x B
14 cm

3 Shapes C and D are similar. Find y and z.

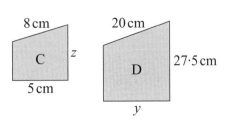

8 cm
C
5 cm
z

20 cm
D
27·5 cm
y

4 Use similar triangles to find x.

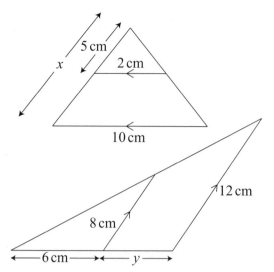

5 Use similar triangles to find y.

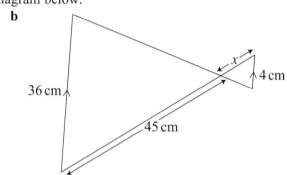

6 Use similar triangles to find x in each diagram below.

a   **b**

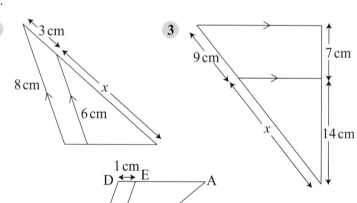

TASK M13.4

In Questions **1** to **3**, find x.

1   **2**   **3**

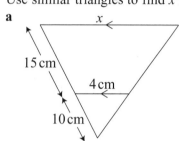

4 Find AB and AE.

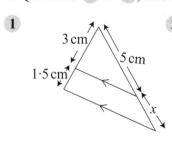

5 **a** *Explain* why triangles PQR and STR are similar.
b Find the length of ST.

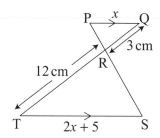

6 Find x and y.

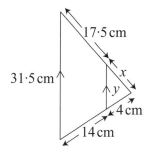

7 Find x.

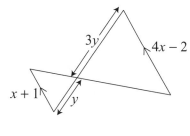

8 Find x and y.

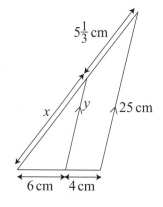

TASK E13.6

1 Find the volume of the larger of these 2 similar cylinders.

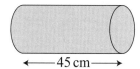
volume = 32 cm³

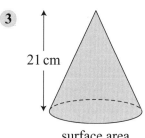

2 These prisms are similar. The total surface area of the smaller prism is 19 cm². Find the total surface area of the larger prism.

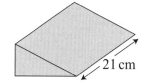

3

surface area = 576 cm²   surface area = 16 cm²

These cones are similar. Find h.

4 A factory makes two footballs and they charge a fixed price *per square metre* of leather that is used to cover the football. If they charge £12 for the football of radius 15 cm, how much do they charge for a football of radius 12 cm?

5 Two triangles are similar. The area of the larger triangle is 6 m^2 and its base is 5 m. How long (to the nearest cm) is the base of the smaller triangle if its area is 1 m^2?

6 The cost of similar bottles of milk is proportional to the *volume*. A bottle which has a radius of 36 mm costs 75 p.
  a What is the price (to the nearest pence) of the bottle with a radius of 45 mm?
  b What is the radius (to 3 sig. figs.) of the bottle which costs £1?

7 These two containers are similar. The ratio of their diameters is 3 : 7. Find the capacity of the smaller container if the larger container has a capacity of 34 litres (give your answer to 3 sig. figs).

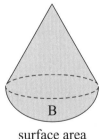

8 A shop sells bars of soap in various sizes, all of which are similar to each other. The shop charges the same amount per cm^3 of soap in each bar. If the bar which is 5 cm long costs 80p then what is the price (to the nearest pence) of the bar which is 8 cm long?

TASK E13.7

1 These two shapes are similar. If the volume of A is 47 cm^3, find:
  a the area ratio
  b the length ratio
  c the volume ratio
  d the volume of B

A
surface area
= 13 cm^2

B
surface area
= 468 cm^2

2 These two hemispheres are similar. If the surface area of Q is 912 cm^3, find
  a the volume ratio
  b the length ratio
  c the area ratio
  d the surface area of P

P
volume
= 8 cm^3

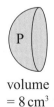

Q
volume
= 512 cm^3

3 Two hexagonal prisms are similar. One has a capacity of 5·4 *l* and the other has a capacity of 6·9 *l*. If the surface area of the smaller one is 19 m², what is the surface area (to 3 sig. figs) of the larger one?

4 A bottle has a surface area of 480 cm² and a volume of 700 cm³. What is the surface area (to 3 sig. figs) of a bottle whose volume is 500 cm³?

5 A towel has a volume of 6100 cm³. The towel shrinks in a tumble drier. It remains a similar shape but its surface area is reduced by 12%. Find the new volume of the towel (to 3 sig. figs).

6 Two crystals are similar. Their surface areas are in the ratio 5 : 9. If the volume of the smaller crystal is 8·7 mm³, find the volume of the larger crystal (to 3 sig. figs).

7 Two similar solid statues are made from the same material. The surface area of the larger statue is 2749 cm² and the smaller statue is 1364 cm². The cost of the material to make the larger statue is £490. What is the cost of the material to make the smaller statue (to the nearest pence)?

DATA 3   14

TASK M14.1

You may use a calculator for this Exercise.

1 For each set of numbers below, find
   i the mean   **ii** the median   **iii** the mode and   **iv** the range
   a 6   10   9   3   16   10   2
   b 8   11   4   8   15   4   16   5   10

2 The ages of the members of a football team are:
   19   27   22   21   24   33   29   26   22   18   31
   Two players are 'sent off' in a match. They are the 29 year-old and the 18 year-old. Find the mean age of the players left on the pitch.

3 Seven people score the following marks in a test:
   30   40   40   40   45   45   96
   Find **a** the mean **b** the median **c** Which average best describes these marks? *Explain why.*

4 In a shooting match, Rose scores:
   8   9   9   9   10   9   9   9   9   10
   Find **a** the mode **b** the mean **c** Which average best describes these scores, the mode or the mean? *Explain why.*

5 ☐ ☐4☐ ☐9☐ ☐ Ross has 5 cards. The 5 cards have a
mean of 7, a median of 7 and a range of 13. What are the 5 numbers on
the cards?

6 The mean average age of 6 people is 37. What is the total of all their ages?

7 The mean weight of 11 people is 63 kg.
   a What is the total weight of all 11 people?
   b One person of weight 83 kg leaves the group.
      Find the mean weight of the remaining 10 people.

8 The mean average salary of 7 people is £26 500. Gemma joins the
group. If she earns £32 100, what is the mean average salary of all
8 people?

9 The mean amount of weekly pocket money for 36 boys is £4·50.
The mean amount of weekly pocket money for 14 girls is £5·50.
Find the mean amount of weekly pocket money for all 50 children.

10 100 people are surveyed about their weekly pay. 50 people from
Banford have mean average pay of £460. 30 people in Darrington have
mean average pay of £340. 20 people from Dalton have mean average
pay equal to the mean average pay of all 100 people. Find the mean
average pay of all 100 people.

TASK M14.2

1 The table below shows the number of drinks some children had during
one day.

Number of drinks	1	2	3	4	5
Frequency	7	12	8	23	29

Find   **a** the modal number of drinks
          b the median number of drinks

2 The 2 tables below show the number of GCSE grade C's obtained by
some students.

Number of C grades	1	2	3	4	5
Frequency	20	38	18	27	24

Boys

Number of C grades	1	2	3	4	5
Frequency	26	20	41	39	67

Girls

   a Find the median number of C grades for the boys.
   b Find the median number of C grades for the girls.
   c Which group has the higher median number of C grades?

3 The table below shows how many times some people ate meat during one week.

Number of times meat eaten	0 to 1	2 to 5	6 to 8	over 8
Frequency	75	51	104	17

Find **a** the modal interval

  b the interval which contains the median

4 Some students from nearby schools are asked how often they go each month to a local skateboard park. The information is shown in the tables below.

Chetley Park School	
Park Visits	Frequency
0 to 1	27
2 to 5	21
6 to 9	15
10 or more	8

Wetton School	
Park Visits	Frequency
0 to 1	19
2 to 5	23
6 to 9	34
10 or more	17

  a For each school, find the interval which contains the median.
  b From which school do students generally go to the skateboard park more often? Explain why you think this.

TASK M14.3

Use a calculator if you need to.

1 Some young people were asked how many different mobile phones they had owned during the last 6 years. The information is shown in the table below.

Number of phones	0	1	2	3	4
Frequency	7	4	12	14	3

  a Find the total number of phones.
  b Find the mean average number of phones.

2 Some people were asked how many computers they had in total in their houses.
  a Find the total number of computers.
  b Find the mean average number of computers per house (give your answer to 1 decimal place).

Number of computers	Frequency
0	16
1	26
2	37
3	20
4	5

3 Some teenagers in 2 areas of a city were asked how many pairs of shoes they owned. The results are shown in the tables below.

Area A

Number of pairs of shoes	1	2	3	4	5	6
Frequency	5	11	28	24	8	3

Area B

Number of pairs of shoes	1	2	3	4	5	6
Frequency	1	6	23	61	42	24

a Work out the mean number of pairs of shoes for each area, giving your answers to one decimal place.

b In which area do your results suggest that teenagers own more pairs of shoes per person?

TASK M14.4

1 Some people were asked how many times they ate out in a restaurant or pub during one month. The information is shown below.

Number of meals (m)	$0 \leqslant m < 2$	$2 \leqslant m < 5$	$5 \leqslant m < 10$	$10 \leqslant m < 20$
Frequency	24	39	16	12

a Estimate the total number of meals.

b Estimate the mean average (give your answer to the nearest whole number)

c *Explain* why your answer is an estimate.

2 The number of goals scored by two hockey teams over the last 15 years is shown in the tables below.

Batton City	
Number of goals (g)	Frequency
$20 \leqslant g < 30$	2
$30 \leqslant g < 40$	3
$40 \leqslant g < 50$	5
$50 \leqslant g < 60$	4
$60 \leqslant g < 70$	1

Chorley Town	
Number of goals (g)	Frequency
$20 \leqslant g < 30$	2
$30 \leqslant g < 40$	6
$40 \leqslant g < 50$	4
$50 \leqslant g < 60$	3
$60 \leqslant g < 70$	0

a Which team has scored the higher mean average number of goals?

b Write down the value of the higher mean average (give your answer to one decimal place).

c What is the *difference* between the mean average number of goals scored by each team?

3 The weights of rugby players in 2 teams are shown in the tables below.

weight w (kg)	$75 \leqslant w < 85$	$85 \leqslant w < 95$	$95 \leqslant w < 100$	$100 \leqslant w < 110$	$110 \leqslant w < 120$
frequency	2	2	3	5	3

Callum hornets

weight w (kg)	$75 \leqslant w < 85$	$85 \leqslant w < 95$	$95 \leqslant w < 100$	$100 \leqslant w < 110$	$110 \leqslant w < 120$
frequency	1	5	2	6	1

Eastham sharks

a Estimate the mean weight for each rugby team (give your answer to one decimal place).

b Which team is the heavier?

TASK M14.5

1 This stem and leaf diagram shows how much money was raised by some children on a sponsored 'silence.'

a Write down the median amount of money.

b What is the range for these amounts of money?

Stem	Leaf
1	7 9
2	4 4 5 8 9 9
3	2 6 6
4	3 8 8 8
5	1 4

Key 2|4 = £24

2 The weights of 22 people were recorded to the nearest kg.

64 71 63 78 82 49 71 65 74 78 53
58 82 66 65 71 87 65 53 72 68 81

a Show this data on a stem and leaf diagram.

b Write down the range of this data.

3 The heights of the players in two hockey teams, the Tampton Trojans and Mallow Town, are shown in the back-to-back stem and leaf diagram.

a Find the median and range for Mallow Town.

b Find the median and range for the Tampton Trojans.

c Write a sentence to compare the heights of the players in each hockey team (use the median and range).

The Tampton Trojans		Mallow Town
	15	6
9 3	16	1 8 8
8 5 5 2 1	17	2 4 7 7
4 4 3	18	3
6	19	0 2

Key 2|17 = 172   Key 18|3 = 183

TASK M14.6

For each set of data below, work out the:
a median   **b** lower quartile   **c** upper quartile   **d** interquartile range

1   3   6   6   7   9   9   9   10   11   12   14   14   16   17   17

2   0·8   0·9   0·4   0·8   0·5   0·4   0·9   1·3   1·2   0·6   0·9

3 $\frac{1}{3}$ $\frac{7}{8}$ $\frac{1}{2}$ $\frac{1}{10}$ $\frac{1}{4}$ $\frac{3}{4}$ $\frac{2}{3}$

4   The cost of the last seven garments of clothing bought by Carl are (in pounds):
     32   7   12   65   28   13   23
     The cost of the last eleven garments of clothing bought by Bron are (in pounds):
     24   6   14   13   29   19   4   81   12   25   17
     a Find the median cost for each person.
     b Find the interquartile range for each person.
     c Use the medians and the interquartile ranges to compare the costs of
        the garments of clothing bought by Carl and Bron.

TASK M14.7

1   Two hundred 17–19 year-olds are asked how many hours of driving practice they have had.
     a Copy the table, adding a cumulative frequency column.
     b Draw a cumulative frequency graph.
     c Use the graph to estimate
        i the median and
        ii the interquartile range.
     d What percentage of these people have had 43 or more hours of driving?

hours of driving (h)	frequency
$0 \leqslant h < 10$	12
$10 \leqslant h < 20$	31
$20 \leqslant h < 30$	59
$30 \leqslant h < 40$	45
$40 \leqslant h < 50$	27
$50 \leqslant h < 60$	18
$60 \leqslant h < 70$	8

2   This cumulative frequency graph shows the weights of 70 children of different ages who play at a local football club.
     Use the graph to estimate:
     a the median weight
     b the lower quartile
     c the upper quartile
     d the interquartile range
     e how many children weighed 78 kg or more?

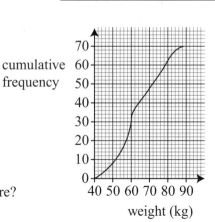

3 Some 18 year-olds planning to go to University are asked if they have saved any money towards it and, if so, how much. The information is shown in the table below:

money saved *m* (£)	frequency
$0 \leqslant m < 500$	34
$500 \leqslant m < 1000$	27
$1000 \leqslant m < 1500$	45
$1500 \leqslant m < 2000$	31
$2000 \leqslant m < 2500$	15
$2500 \leqslant m < 3000$	8
$3000 \leqslant m < 3500$	7
$3500 \leqslant m < 4000$	5

a Copy the table, adding a cumulative frequency column.
b Draw a cumulative frequency graph.
c Use the graph to estimate
   i the median and
   ii the interquartile range.
d What percentage of these 18 year-olds have saved more than £2400?

TASK M14.8

1 Some people were asked about the age of their fathers when they were born. The information is shown in the box plot below:

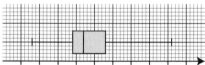

15 20 25 30 35 40 45 50 55 60 age (years)

Find **a** the median
       b the range
       c the lower quartile
       d the upper quartile
       e the interquartile range

2 Some people were asked how many days they had been absent from work for illness in the last year. The results are shown in the table opposite. Draw a box plot to show this data.

	days off for illness
lowest value	0
highest value	23
median	7
lower quartile	5
upper quartile	12

3 The box plots below show the best times for a group of boys and girls when running the 100 m sprint.

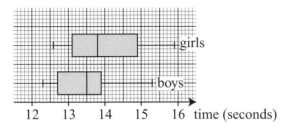

Use the medians, ranges and interquartile ranges to compare the times for the boys and girls.

4 Two groups of men and women were asked how long they spent on average taking a bath. A summary of the findings is shown below.

	time spent by men (minutes)	time spent by women (minutes)
lowest value	3	5
highest value	55	56
median	18	19
lower quartile	11	10
upper quartile	25	25

a Draw a box plot for each group of people.
b Compare the time spent in the bath by these groups of men and women.

5 This cumulative frequency graph shows the average time per night spent on homework by pupils in class 11X.

cumulative
frequency

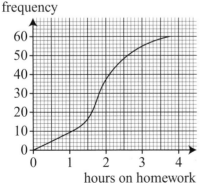

hours on homework

The box plot below shows the average time per night spent on homework by pupils in class 11Y.

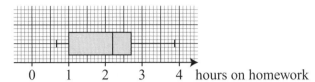

0   1   2   3   4   hours on homework

Comment on the differences in the time spent on homework by pupils in the two classes.

TASK E14.1

1 A number of schoolchildren were asked how long they took from getting out of bed to leaving for school on an average morning. The information is shown in the table opposite.

a Work out the frequency density for each class interval.

b Draw a histogram to illustrate this data.

time t (minutes)	frequency
$10 \leqslant t < 15$	25
$15 \leqslant t < 25$	70
$25 \leqslant t < 30$	60
$30 \leqslant t < 40$	80
$40 \leqslant t < 60$	100
$60 \leqslant t < 90$	60

2 The table below shows the ages at which a number of people living in a village took out pension plans.

age (years)	20–24	25–34	35–39	40–44	45–59	60–69
frequency	22	32	28	49	99	37

a Explain why the '25–34' class when written as an inequality is $25 \leqslant A < 35$ where A is the age.

b Explain why the frequency density for the '25–34' class is 3·2.

c Draw a histogram to illustrate this data.

3 The heights of a number of students in a school are recorded (to the nearest cm). The information is shown below.

height (cm)	140–149	150–153	154–159	160–163	164–171	172–181	182–199
frequency	33	6	27	26	68	57	36

a Explain why the '154–159' class when written as an inequality is $153·5 \leqslant h < 159·5$ where h is the height.

b Explain why the frequency density for the '154–159' class is 4·5.

c Draw a histogram.

126

TASK E14.2

1 This histogram shows the number of hours of exercise taken by a group of people each week.

   a Copy and complete the frequency table below.

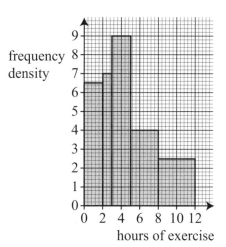

frequency density

hours of exercise

hours of exercise (h)	frequency
$0 \leqslant h < 2$	
$2 \leqslant h < 3$	
$3 \leqslant h < 5$	
$5 \leqslant h < 8$	
$8 \leqslant h < 12$	

   b What is the total frequency?

2 This histogram shows the ages of some members of a drama group. Copy and complete the frequency table below.

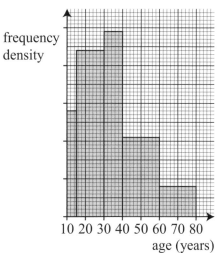

frequency density

age (years)

age A (years)	frequency
$10 \leqslant A < 15$	
$15 \leqslant A < 30$	
$30 \leqslant A < 40$	
$40 \leqslant A < 60$	42
$60 \leqslant A < 80$	

3 This histogram shows the percentage of rubbish which is recycled by households in the village of Grensham.

   a Copy and complete the frequency table below.

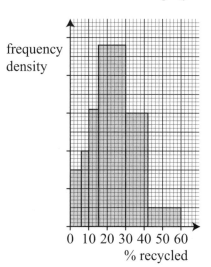

frequency density

% recycled

% recycled R	frequency
$0 \leqslant R < 6$	
$6 \leqslant R < 10$	
$10 \leqslant R < 15$	31
$15 \leqslant R < 30$	
$30 \leqslant R < 42$	
$42 \leqslant R < 60$	

b What is the total frequency?

c What percentage of the houses recycle between 10% and 30% of their rubbish (give your answer to 1 dec. place)?

4 The unfinished histogram and table below show the annual salaries of the employees of a particular company.

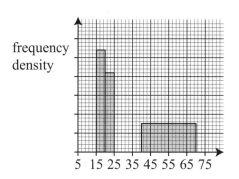

frequency density

salary s (£1000's)	frequency
$5 \leqslant s < 15$	175
$15 \leqslant s < 20$	
$20 \leqslant s < 25$	110
$25 \leqslant s < 40$	285
$40 \leqslant s < 70$	

a Use the information shown on the histogram to copy and complete the table.

b Use the information shown in the table to copy and complete the histogram.

c What percentage of the employees earn more than £25 000? (give your answer to 1 dec. place)

TASK E14.3

1 The table below shows the number of e-mails received by children in class 10P during January.

number of e-mails	0–10	11–20	21–30	31–40	41–50	51–60
frequency	7	4	9	6	6	2

The box plot below shows the number of e-mails received by children in class 10Q during January.

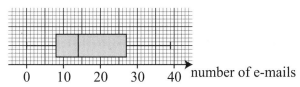

number of e-mails

a Draw a cumulative frequency graph for the number of e-mails received by children in class 10P.

b Find the median and interquartile range from this cumulative frequency graph. Use these to compare the distribution of the number of e-mails for class 10P and 10Q.

2 Some 8 year-olds and some 18 year-olds are asked how many Christmas presents they had last Christmas.

a Estimate the mean average for the 8 year-olds.

b Estimate the mean average for the 18 year-olds.

c Compare the number of Christmas presents received by the 8 year-olds and the 18 year-olds.

8 year-olds	
0 to 8	6
9 to 16	31
17 to 24	48
25 to 32	10
33 to 40	3
41 to 48	2

18 year-olds	
0 to 8	34
9 to 16	26
17 to 24	9
25 to 32	5
33 to 40	1
41 to 48	0

3 The histogram below shows the ages in country A at which a sample of women gave birth to their first child.

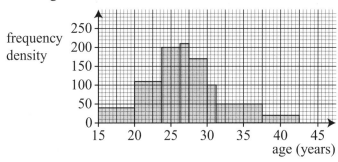

The table below shows the ages in country B at which a sample of women gave birth to their first child.

age A (years)	$15 \leq A < 18$	$18 \leq A < 20$	$20 \leq A < 21$	$21 \leq A < 23$	$23 \leq A < 28$	$28 \leq A < 35$
frequency	240	320	240	460	500	140

a Using the same scale as the above histogram, draw a histogram to illustrate the data for country B.

b Compare the distribution of the ages at which women gave birth to their first child in countries A and B.

ALGEBRA 4   16

TASK M16.1

Write down the inequalities shown below:

1 a    b   c

2 Write down all the integer values (whole numbers) of x which satisfy each inequality below.

a $4 \leqslant x \leqslant 7$ b $0 < x \leqslant 5$ c $-4 \leqslant x < -1$ d $-6 < x < 1$

3 Solve the inequalities below:

a $3x + 2 > 17$ b $2(x + 3) < 18$ c $6x - 4 > 3x + 17$

d $\frac{x}{2} > -5$ e $6(x - 2) \geqslant 24$ f $\frac{x}{4} - 3 \leqslant 3$

4 Find the range of values of x which satisfy each inequality below and show each answer on a number line.

a $3 + x < 6$ b $2 \leqslant x - 1 \leqslant 4$ c $-2 \leqslant 3x + 4 < 7$

5 Write down the greatest positive integer n which satisfies each inequality below:

a $4 - 9n > -23$ b $\frac{4n + 3}{7} \leqslant 5$ c $-1 - 5n \geqslant -8$

6 Solve the inequalities below:

a $2 - 3x > 4 - x$ b $5(x - 1) \geqslant 2(4x + 3)$ c $1 \leqslant \frac{2x - 3}{5} \leqslant 5$

TASK M16.2

1 Solve $x^2 \leqslant 16$ and show the answer on a number line.

2 Solve $2x^2 < 2$ and show the answer on a number line.

3 Solve the inequalities below:

a $n^2 > 36$ b $y^2 \leqslant 64$ c $x^2 \geqslant 169$ d $5m^2 > 45$

e $3z^2 - 5 < 7$ f $8b^2 + 2 \leqslant 34$ g $242 - 2a^2 < 0$ h $7(x^2 - 3) \leqslant 42$

4 Solve $67 - 4n^2 > 17 - 2n^2$ and show the answer on a number line.

5 Solve $2(3y^2 - 1) \geqslant 88 - 4y^2$ and show the answer on a number line.

6 Solve $(x - 3)^2 \leqslant 4$ and show the answer on a number line.

TASK M16.3

1 Write down the inequality which describes the shaded region.

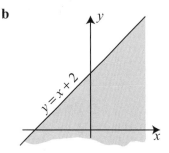

a $y = 3$

b $y = x + 2$

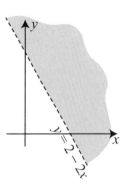

2 For each shaded region, write down the 3 inequalities which describe it.

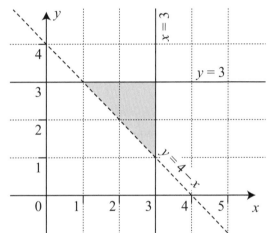

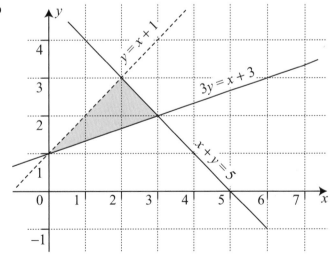

3 Draw graphs to show the regions given by the inequalities below:
   a $2 \leqslant y \leqslant 5$ **b** $y < x + 3$ **c** $3x + 4y \geqslant 12$

4 Draw a graph to show the region defined by all 3 inequalities given below. Shade the required region.
   $y \geqslant x - 1$ $5x + 6y \leqslant 30$ $x > 1$

5 By finding the equation of each boundary line, write down the 3 inequalities which describe this shaded region.

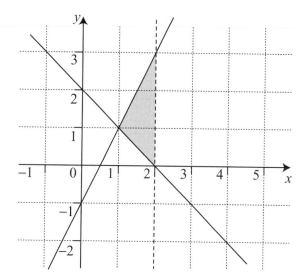

6 a Draw x and y-axes from -3 to 5.

  b If x and y are integers only, mark with a ✕ all co-ordinates which lie in the region defined by the 3 inequalities below.

  $y > x - 2$ $x > -2$ $x + y \leqslant 3$

  (You should end up plotting 16 crosses)

TASK M16.4

1 a and b are lengths.

$H = ab^2$ Is this a formula for a length, area or volume?

2 r is a length.

$P = 4\pi r$ Is this a formula for a length, area or volume?

3 Each letter below is a length. For each expression write down if it represents a length, area or volume.

a $3h$	**b** x^2	**c** $4xy$	**d** πabc	**e** $3\pi x$
f πxy	**g** $6\pi r$	**h** $3x^2y$	**i** $4rh$	**j** $5r$
k $4xyz$	**l** $7x$	**m** $3\pi ab$	**n** $2\pi a^2$	**o** $5y^3$

4 a, b and c are lengths.

Which of the formulas below represent a volume?

$\boxed{6a^3}$ $\boxed{\pi ac}$ $\boxed{7\pi b}$ $\boxed{\pi b^2 c}$ $\boxed{2ab^2}$

TASK M16.5

1 a and b are lengths.

$P = 4\pi ab + 9b^2$

Is this a formula for a length, area, volume or does it have no meaning?

2 Each letter below is a length. For each expression write down if it represents a length, area, volume or has no meaning.

a $4x + 3y$

b $2m^2 - 5n$

c $3x^2y + \pi x^3$

d $\pi ab - 5a^2$

e $5pq + 6pq^2$

f $3xyz - 2\pi y^2$

g $\pi(a - b)$

h $5a(b^2 - 2ab)$

i $3\pi abc + 4b^2c$

j $\dfrac{\pi r^3}{l}$

k $4x(\pi x - y)$

l $3m(\pi m^3 + 4mn)$

m $\dfrac{2\pi a^3}{\pi}$

n $\dfrac{x^3 - y^3}{x}$

o $2r(3rl + 5r)$

p $\dfrac{\pi a(3a - 4b)}{6b}$

3 x and y are lengths. Which of the formulas below can be used for an area?

$$7x(3x - \pi y)$$
A

$$3xy + 2\pi y$$
B

$$\dfrac{4xy^3}{3\pi y}$$
C

$$2\pi x^2 - 5xy$$
D

$$\dfrac{2x(y^2 + 3x^2)}{5\pi y}$$
E

4 Kat has found a formula for a length:

$$P = \dfrac{5r^{\Box}(3h + 2r)}{\pi h^2}$$

What number belongs in the box?

5 Here are 9 expressions:

$$3a(b + c) \qquad 4b^2(3a - c) \qquad 2b^2(\pi a + ab)$$
$$\pi a^2b - 6a^3 \qquad \dfrac{\pi b^2}{a} + 6\pi b \qquad \dfrac{3abc(4a - b)}{9b^2}$$
$$4a^2 + \pi b \qquad \dfrac{\pi b^3c}{5a} \qquad \dfrac{5c(\pi a^2 + 3ac)}{\pi bc}$$

a and b are lengths. Write down which formulas represent
a area   **b** volume   **c** length

TASK E16.1

1 Write down whether each statement is true or false.

a $\dfrac{3mn - n^2}{mn} = \dfrac{3m - n}{m}$

b $\dfrac{x^2 + y^2}{xy} = x + y$

c $\dfrac{a^2 - 9}{3a^2} = -3$

d $\dfrac{4x^2}{x + 2} = 2x$

e $\dfrac{a^2 + 3a}{ab} = \dfrac{a + 3}{b}$

f $\dfrac{4m^2 - n^2}{2m} = 2m - n^2$

2 Simplify

a $\dfrac{6a}{12b}$

b $\dfrac{x^2}{xy}$

c $\dfrac{9mn}{12m^2}$

d $\dfrac{a + b}{ab}$

e $\dfrac{12x - 8y}{4}$

f $\dfrac{ab + ac}{ad}$

g $\dfrac{3x + 7y}{6x + 14y}$

h $\dfrac{4m^2}{8m - 20mn}$

3 Simplify these fractions by cancelling as far as possible.

a $\dfrac{2x^2 - 6x}{2x}$ **b** $\dfrac{10ab + 5b^2}{6a + 3b}$ **c** $\dfrac{12mn - 8m^2}{3mn - 2m^2}$ **d** $\dfrac{3a^2 - 9ab}{a^2 + 3ab}$

e $\dfrac{x^2 + 4x + 3}{x^2 + 3x}$ **f** $\dfrac{x^2 + 2x - 8}{2x^2 - 4x}$ **g** $\dfrac{n^2 - 6n}{n^2 - 3n - 18}$ **h** $\dfrac{a^2 + 3a - 4}{a^2 - 16}$

i $\dfrac{n^2 + 8n + 15}{n^2 + 3n - 10}$ **j** $\dfrac{a^2 - 9}{a(a + 3)}$ **k** $\dfrac{2w^2 + 3w + 1}{4w^2 - 1}$ **l** $\dfrac{6x^2 - x - 2}{3x^2 + 7x - 6}$

TASK E16.2

Simplify

1 $\dfrac{4a}{b} \times \dfrac{b}{a}$ **2** $\dfrac{x}{y} \times \dfrac{y}{x}$ **3** $\dfrac{6a^2}{3b} \times \dfrac{3b}{9a}$

4 $\dfrac{3x - 2}{4} \times \dfrac{8x + 3}{9x - 6}$ **5** $\dfrac{5m}{4n} \div \dfrac{3}{2n}$ **6** $\dfrac{2x - 1}{4y} \div \dfrac{6x - 3}{y^2}$

7 Show that $\dfrac{x + 3}{x^2 - 9} \times \dfrac{x^2 - x - 6}{x^2 + 3x + 2}$ is equivalent to $\dfrac{4x - 12}{x^2 - 3x - 4} \div \dfrac{4x^2 - 12x}{x^2 - 4x}$

Simplify as far as possible.

8 $\dfrac{x^2 + 4x + 3}{5x + 15} \times \dfrac{x^2 - 4x}{x^2 - 3x - 4}$ **9** $\dfrac{a^2 + 5a + 6}{a^2 + 3a} \times \dfrac{a^2 + 5a - 6}{a^2 + a - 2}$

10 $\dfrac{n^2 - 5n}{n^2 - n - 2} \times \dfrac{n^2 - 4}{n^2 - 3n - 10}$ **11** $\dfrac{3a^2}{a^2 - 1} \times \dfrac{a^2 + 6a - 7}{a^2 + 7a}$

12 $\dfrac{m^2 - 3m}{m^2 + 4m} \div \dfrac{m^2 + 5m}{m^2 + 9m + 20}$ **13** $\dfrac{x^2 - x - 12}{x^2 - 6x + 8} \div \dfrac{x^2 + 4x + 3}{x^2 + 3x - 10}$

14 $\dfrac{b^2 + 6b - 16}{b^2 - 6b + 8} \div \dfrac{b^2 + 11b + 24}{b^2 - 8b + 16}$ **15** $\dfrac{n^2 - 12n + 32}{3n^2 - 24n} \times \dfrac{7n^2 + 28n}{n^2 - 16}$

16 $\dfrac{3x^2 - 11x - 4}{5x^2 - 16x + 3} \div \dfrac{6x^2 + 11x + 3}{10x^2 + 13x - 3}$

TASK E16.3

Simplify

1 $\dfrac{a}{4} + \dfrac{a}{3}$ **2** $\dfrac{3m}{4} - \dfrac{2n}{3}$ **3** $\dfrac{x}{y} + \dfrac{2y}{x}$ **4** $\dfrac{4}{5m} + \dfrac{2}{3n}$

5 $\dfrac{2}{3a} - \dfrac{1}{7b}$ **6** $\dfrac{n + 3}{2} + \dfrac{n + 4}{5}$ **7** $\dfrac{a + 6}{3} - \dfrac{a}{4}$ **8** $\dfrac{5x}{8} + \dfrac{x - 3}{6}$

Write as a single fraction:

9 $\dfrac{5}{x + 2} + \dfrac{3}{x + 4}$ **10** $\dfrac{7}{n + 5} + \dfrac{2}{n + 3}$ **11** $\dfrac{4}{y + 6} - \dfrac{3}{y + 5}$

12 $\dfrac{8}{m + 1} - \dfrac{3}{m - 4}$ **13** $\dfrac{4}{2a + 3} - \dfrac{1}{4a - 1}$ **14** $\dfrac{9}{a - b} + \dfrac{4}{b - a}$

Simplify

15 $\dfrac{3}{(x+2)(x+3)} + \dfrac{4}{x+2}$

16 $\dfrac{6}{n+5} + \dfrac{2}{n^2+3n-10}$

17 $\dfrac{3}{w-1} - \dfrac{15}{w^2+3w-4}$

18 $\dfrac{8}{m-4} + \dfrac{3}{m^2-16}$

19 $\dfrac{2}{y^2-9} + \dfrac{1}{y^2+9y+18}$

20 $\dfrac{5}{x^2+7x+12} + \dfrac{4}{x^2+5x+4}$

TASK E16.4

1 Solve

a $\dfrac{x+4}{7} + \dfrac{x}{3} = 2$

b $m - \dfrac{15}{m} = 14$

c $\dfrac{n-5}{3} + \dfrac{n+2}{2} = 16$

2 Show that $\dfrac{2}{x-1} + \dfrac{1}{x+4} = 2$ is equivalent to $2x^2 + 3x - 15 = 0$

3 Show that $\dfrac{2}{x+5} + \dfrac{3}{x+1} = 6$ is equivalent to $6x^2 + 31x + 13 = 0$

4 Solve these equations. Give the answers to 3 significant figures when necessary.

a $\dfrac{3}{x} + \dfrac{2}{x+3} = 1$

b $\dfrac{3}{m+1} + \dfrac{8}{m+2} = 3$

c $\dfrac{6}{w+3} + \dfrac{5}{w-2} = 9$

d $\dfrac{4}{x-3} - \dfrac{1}{x+1} = 2$

5 A motorbike travels 50 m at a speed v which is greater than 15 m/s. It then travels 200 m at a speed of 5 m/s less than its speed for the first 50 m. The motorbike takes 12 seconds to complete the 250 m.
   a Write down an equation involving its speed v and show that it simplifies to $6v^2 - 155v + 125 = 0$.
   b Solve this equation to find v.

6 The perimeter of this rectangle is 4 cm.
   Write down an equation involving x and solve it to find x.

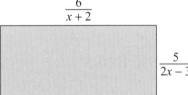

TASK E16.5

1 Use algebra to prove that the sum of 2 odd numbers is even.

2 Prove that $(n+2)^2 - (n+1)^2 = 2n+3$.

3 Prove that $(n+1)^2 + (n+3)^2 - 10 = 2n(n+4)$.

4 Prove that the difference between the squares of 2 consecutive odd numbers is a multiple of 8.

5 Prove that the sum of the squares of consecutive integers is odd.

6 A sequence is formed as follows:

$$1 \times 4 = 4$$
$$2 \times 5 = 10$$
$$3 \times 6 = 18$$
$$4 \times 7 = 28$$

a Write down a formula for the $n^{\text{th.}}$ term.
b Explain why the formula for the $(n + 1)^{\text{th.}}$ term is $(n + 1)(n + 4)$.
c Prove that the difference between two consecutive terms in the sequence is $2n + 4$.

7 Prove that the sum of the squares of three consecutive odd numbers less 35 is a multiple of 12.

8 $n^2 + n$ is always an even number if n is a positive integer. Prove that the difference between the cubes of consecutive positive integers is always 1 more than a multiple of 6.

SHAPE 5   17

TASK M17.1

1 The model of a statue is made using a scale of $1 : 40$. If the statue is 3·2 m tall, how tall is the model (give your answer in cm)?

2 A park is 5 cm long on a map whose scale is $1 : 40\,000$. Find the actual length (in km) of the park.

3 Copy and complete the table below.

Map length	Scale	Real length
7 cm	1 : 60	m
5 cm	1 : 2000	m
8 cm	1 : 50 000	km
cm	1 : 100 000	3 km
cm	1 : 4000	320 m
cm	1 : 5 000 000	125 km

4 The distance between two towns is 25 km. How far apart will they be on a map of scale $1 : 500\,000$?

5 A plan of a house is made using a scale of 1 : 30. The width of the house on the plan is 40 cm. What is the real width of the house (give your answer in metres)?

6 A map has a scale of 1 : 60 000.
   a What is the actual area (in km²) of the shape ABCD shown opposite?
   b What is the real size of ∠ABC?

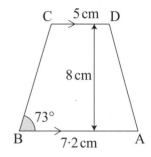

TASK M17.2

1 Draw ∠ABC = 70°.
Construct the bisector of the angle.
Use a protractor to check that each half of the angle now measures 35°.

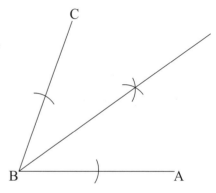

2 Draw any angle and construct the bisector of this angle.

3 Draw a horizontal line AB of length 7 cm. Construct the perpendicular bisector of AB. Check that each half of the line measures 3·5 cm exactly.

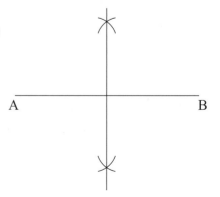

4 Draw any vertical line. Construct the perpendicular bisector of the line.

5   Construct accurately the diagrams below:

    a   Measure angle x and side y.

                                                b   Measure angle x and angle y.

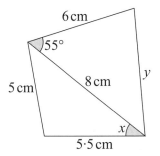

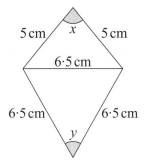

6   **a**   Draw PQ and QR at right angles to each other as shown.

    b   Construct the perpendicular bisector of QR.

    c   Construct the perpendicular bisector of PQ.

    d   The two perpendicular bisectors meet at a point (label this as S). Measure QS.

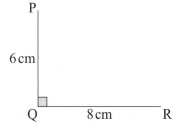

TASK M17.3

1   Construct an equilateral triangle with each side equal to 7 cm.

2   Construct an angle of 60°.

3   **a**   Draw a line 8 cm long and mark the point A as shown.

               5 cm   A   3 cm

    b   Construct an angle of 90° at A.

4   **a**   Draw a line 10 cm long and mark the point B on the line as shown.

               4 cm   B   6 cm

    b   Construct an angle of 45° at B.

5   Construct a right-angled triangle ABC, where $\angle ABC = 90°$, BC = 6 cm and $\angle ACB = 60°$. Measure the length of AB.

6   Construct this triangle with ruler and compasses only. Measure x.

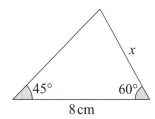

7 Draw any line and any point A.
Construct the perpendicular from the point A
to the line.

• A

_____

TASK M17.4

You will need a ruler and a pair of compasses.

1 Draw the locus of all points which are less than or equal to 3 cm
from a point A.

2 Draw the locus of all points which are exactly 4 cm from a
point B.

3 Draw the locus of all points which are exactly 4 cm
from the line PQ.

P————————————Q
5 cm

4 A triangular garden has a tree at the corner B.
The whole garden is made into a lawn except for anywhere
less than or equal to 6 m from the tree. Using a scale of
1 cm for 3 m, draw the garden and shade in the lawn.

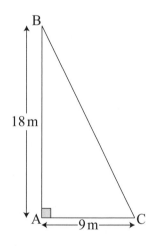

5 In a field a goat is attached by a rope to a peg P as shown.
The rope is 30 m long. Using a scale of 1 cm for 10 m,
copy the diagram then shade the area that the goat
can roam in.

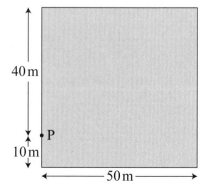

6 Draw the square opposite.
Draw the locus of all the points *outside* the square which
are 3 cm from the edge of the square.

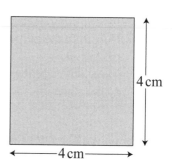

4 cm

←—— 4 cm ——→

7 Each square is 1 m wide. The shaded
area shows a building.
A guard dog is attached by a chain
5 m long to the point A on the outside
of the building.
Draw the diagram on squared paper
then shade the region the dog can cover.

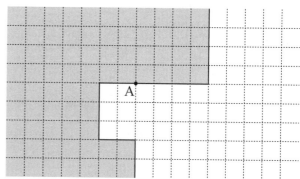

TASK M17.5

You will need a ruler and a pair of compasses.

1 Construct the locus of points which are the same distance from the
lines AB and BC (the bisector of angle B).

A

B ————————— C

2 Faye wants to lay a path in her garden that is always the
same distance from KL and KN.
Using a scale of 1 cm for 10 m, draw the garden and construct
a line to show where the path will be laid.

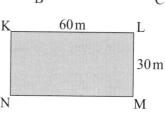

K ——— 60 m ——— L

30 m

N   M

3 Construct the locus of points which are
equidistant (the same distance) from M and N.

M •------------------------• N
7 cm

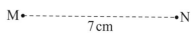

4 Draw A and B 7 cm apart.

A•   •B

A radar at A has a range of 150 km and a radar at B has a range of
90 km. Using a scale of 1 cm for every 30 km, show the area which can
be covered by both radars at the same time.

5 Draw one copy of this diagram.
   a Construct the perpendicular bisector of FG and the bisector of ∠FGH.
   b Make with a ✗ the point which is equidistant from F and G as well as the same distance from the lines FG and GH.

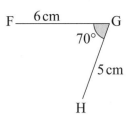

6 Draw the line QR then draw the locus of all the points P such that ∠QPR = 90°.

7 Draw one copy of triangle ABC and show on it:
   a the perpendicular bisector of QR.
   b the bisector of ∠PRQ.
   c the locus of points nearer to PR than to QR *and* nearer to R than to Q.

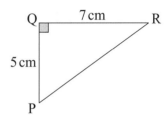

TASK E17.1

1 **a** Draw a graph of $y = \sin\theta$ for values of θ from 0° to 360° using intervals of 30°.

Use the graph to decide which of the statements below are true:
   b $\sin 150° = \sin 60°$
   c $\sin 330° = -\sin 30°$
   d $\sin 225° = \sin 45°$
   e $\sin 135° = \sin 45°$

2 This is part of the graph of $y = \cos x$.
Write down the co-ordinates of the points A, B, C and D.

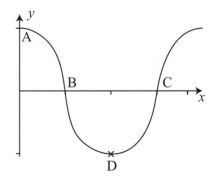

3 Look at the graph in Question **2**. *Explain* why cos 240° cannot equal cos 60°.

4 Write down the lowest possible value of cos x.

5 Write down the greatest possible value of sin x.

6 How often does the sine curve repeat itself?

7 By considering the graph of $y = \tan x$ between values of x from $0°$ to $720°$, how many times will the value of $\tan x$ equal $2·5$?

TASK E17.2

Use the symmetry of the graphs of $y = \sin x$ and $y = \cos x$ to answer the following Questions, giving your answers to the nearest degree.

1 If $\sin 53° = 0·799$, find another angle whose sine is $0·799$.

2 If $\cos 220° = -0·766$, find another angle whose cosine is $-0·766$.

3 Write down another angle which has the same cosine as
 a $39°$ **b** $47°$ **c** $171°$ **d** $108°$

4 Express the following in terms of the sine, cosine or tangent of an acute angle (the first one is done for you):
 a $\cos 320° = \cos 40°$ **b** $\cos 160°$ **c** $\sin 173°$ **d** $\cos 346°$
 e $\sin 294°$ **f** $\sin 219°$ **g** $\tan 247°$ **h** $\cos 162°$

5 Find two solutions between $0°$ and $360°$ for each of the following:
 a $\cos x = 0·7$ **b** $\sin x = 0·18$ **c** $\sin x = -0·93$
 d $\cos x = 0·84$ **e** $\cos x = -0·62$ **f** $\sin x = -0·447$

6 Solve $5\cos x = 1$ for x-values between $0°$ and $360°$.

7 Solve $2\sin x = -\sqrt{3}$ for x-values between $0°$ and $360°$.

8 Write down 3 values of x for which $\sin x = -0·5$.

9 This is part of the graph of
 $y = 2\cos x + 3$
 Use your calculator to find
 two exact values of x such that
 $2\cos x + 3 = 2$

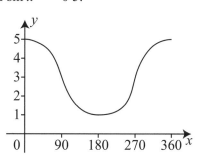

TASK E17.3

1 On squared paper, sketch
 a $f(x) + 1$
 b $-f(x)$
 c $f(x + 1)$
 d $f(x) - 1$

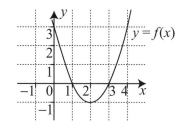

2 On squared paper, sketch

   a $g(x - 2)$

   b $g(x) + 3$

   c $g(-x)$

   d $g(x + 3)$

   e $-g(x)$

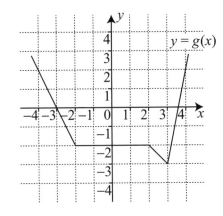

3 $f(x)$ has a minimum point at $(2, -1)$. Write down the co-ordinates of the minimum point for:

   a $f(x + 4)$ **b** $-f(x)$ **c** $f(x-1)$ **d** $f(-x)$

4   **a** Sketch $y = \cos x$ for $0 \leqslant x \leqslant 360°$

    b Sketch $y = \cos (x + 90°)$

    c Sketch $y = 2 + \cos x$

5 Express $g(x)$ in terms of $f(x)$.

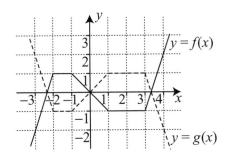

TASK E17.4

1 On squared paper, sketch

   a $y = 2f(x)$

   b $y = f(3x)$

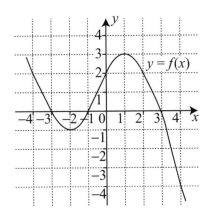

2 On squared paper, sketch

   a $y = g(2x)$

   b $y = 2g(x)$

   c $y = \frac{1}{2}g(x)$

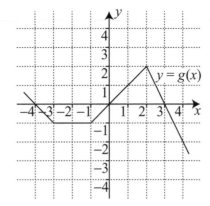

3 Sketch $y = \sin 2x$ for $0 \leqslant x \leqslant 360°$.

4 Sketch $y = 4\cos x$ for $0 \leqslant x \leqslant 360°$.

5 $f(x)$ has a maximum point at $(-4, 6)$. Write down the co-ordinates of the maximum point for:

   a $\frac{1}{2}f(x)$ **b** $f(4x)$ **c** $f\left(\frac{1}{2}x\right)$ **d** $3f(x)$

6 Describe the transformation which changes $y = \cos x$ into $y = \cos 3x$.

7 The graph $y = x^2 - x$ is stretched by a factor of $\frac{1}{2}$ parallel to the x-axis. Write down the equation of the new graph.

TASK E17.5

1 **a** Sketch $y = x^2 - 3$

    b On the same graph, sketch $y = (x + 2)^2 - 3$

2 **a** Sketch $y = 2^x$

    b On the same graph, sketch $y = 2^{-x}$

3 On squared paper, sketch

   a $y = -f(x)$

   b $y = -f(x) - 1$

   c $y = f(-x)$

   d $y = \frac{1}{2}f(x)$

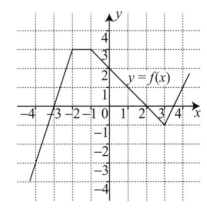

4 $g(x)$ has a minimum point at $(2, 8)$. Write down the co-ordinates of the minimum point for:

   a $g(x + 4)$ **b** $g(x + 4) - 3$ **c** $-g(x)$ **d** $6 - g(x)$

5 The graph of $y = \cos x$ is reflected in the x-axis then translated through $\begin{pmatrix} 0 \\ 3 \end{pmatrix}$. Write down the equation of the new curve drawn.

6 The graph of $y = \sin x$ is stretched by a factor of $\frac{1}{4}$ parallel to the x-axis then translated through $\begin{pmatrix} 0 \\ -2 \end{pmatrix}$. Write down the equation of the curve drawn.

7 On squared paper, sketch
  a $y = 2f(x)$
  b $y = f(x + 2)$
  c $y = 2f(x + 2)$
  d $y = \frac{1}{2}f(x - 1)$

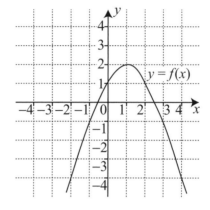

8 The graph of $y = (x + 1)^2 - 3(x + 1)$ is drawn by using the graph of $y = x^2 - 3x$. Describe the transformation.

SHAPE 6   18

TASK M18.1

1 Draw and label the plan and a side elevation for:
  a a cuboid   **b** a cone

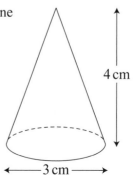

2 How many more cubes are needed to make this shape into a cuboid?

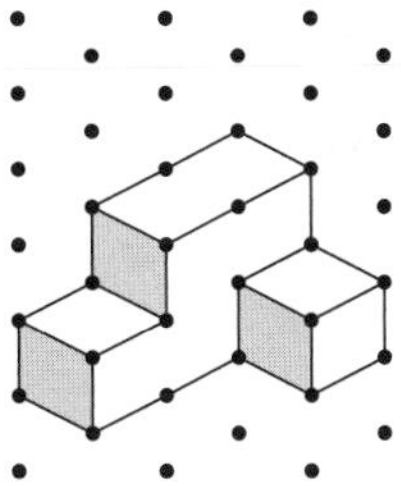

3 Draw this object from a *different view*.

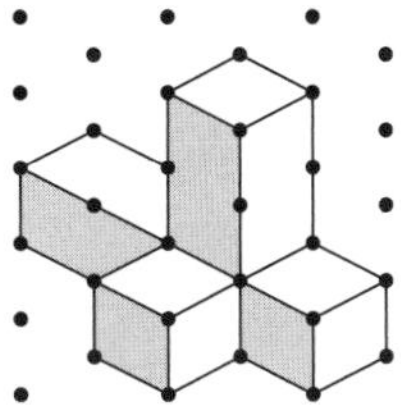

4 You are given the plan and two elevations of an object. Draw each object (on isometric paper if you wish to).

a front elevation

plan view

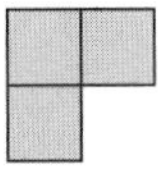

side elevation

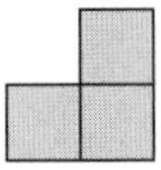

b front elevation

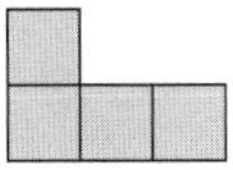

plan view

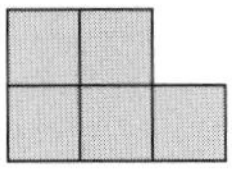

side elevation

c front elevation

plan view

side elevation

d front elevation

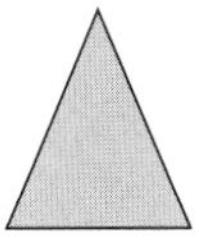

plan view

side elevation

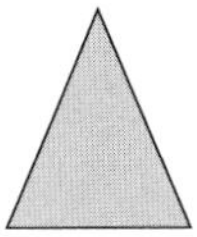

5 Draw a front elevation, plan view and side elevation of each solid below:

a

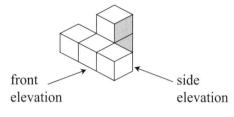

front elevation

side elevation

b

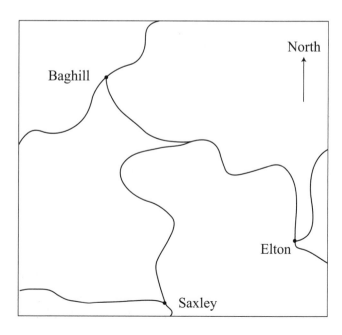

2 cm

3 cm

←2 cm→

TASK M18.2

1 4 rabbits escape from their run and race off in the directions shown. On what bearing does each rabbit race?

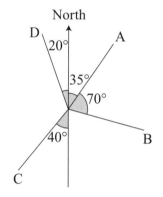

North

D

20°

A

35°

70°

40°

B

C

Remember: a bearing is measured clockwise from the North

2 Use a protractor to measure the bearing of:
   a Elton *from Saxley*
   b Elton *from Baghill*
   c Saxley *from Baghill*
   d Baghill *from Elton*
   e Saxley *from Elton*
   f Baghill *from Saxley*

North

Baghill

Elton

Saxley

Note – the remaining Questions need to be *calculated*. Do not use a protractor. Give answers to one decimal place when appropriate.

3 A plane flies 80 km north and 47 km west. What is the bearing from its original position to its new position?

4 Ken runs 5 km east from his home then 8 km north. On what bearing is he to run home if he is to take the shortest route?

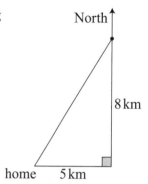

5 B is on a bearing of 305° from C.
  a Find the length of BD.
  b Find the bearing of
    A from B if AD = 4 km.

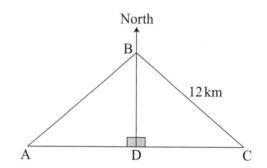

6 Find the bearing of:
  a P from Q
  b R from Q

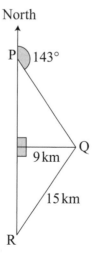

TASK M18.3

Give answers in this Exercise to one decimal place when appropriate.

1 Ben is standing 90 m from the foot of a flagpole. The flagpole is 11 m tall. What is the angle of elevation of the top of the flagpole from Ben?

2 Rosa is standing on the top of a hill looking down at her village. The angle of depression of the top of her house is 7°. If she is 163 m higher than the top of her house, what is the horizontal distance of Rosa from her house?

3 Harry is standing on top of a castle keep, 29 m tall. A friend is standing on the ground below, 70 m from the foot of the castle keep. What is the angle of depression of the friend from Harry?

4 A camera is placed on a table to film a church. The angle of elevation from the camera to the top of a flagpole on the church tower is 5°. Using the measurements shown, what is the horizontal distance from the flagpole to the camera?

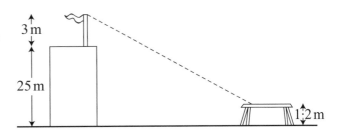

5 The angle of elevation of a bird from an observation point on the ground is 6·7°. If the horizontal distance of the bird from the observation point is 230 m, how high is the bird above the observation point?

6 The angles of elevation of the front of two tall buildings from a point A is shown in the diagram opposite. What is the difference in the heights of the two buildings?

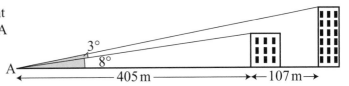

7 A telegraph pole stands on a line joining two points P and Q on the ground. The telegraph pole is 9 m tall. The angle of depression of the top of the pole to point P is 4°. The angle of depression of the top of the pole to point Q is 7°. What is the horizontal distance between P and Q?

TASK M18.4

You may use a calculator.

1 A has co-ordinates (0, 4, 5). Write down the co-ordinates of B, C, D, E, F and G.

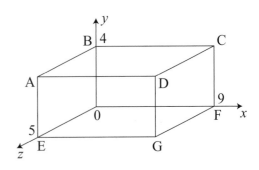

2 Each side of this cube is 2 units long.
   a Write down the co-ordinates of the vertices (corners) O, P, Q, R, S, T, U and V.
   b Calculate the length of QU.

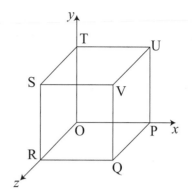

3 OABCDE is a triangular prism. The perpendicular height of triangle ABE is 8 units.
   a Write down the co-ordinates of the vertices O, A, B, C, D, E.
   b Find the co-ordinates of the midpoint of the diagonal AC.

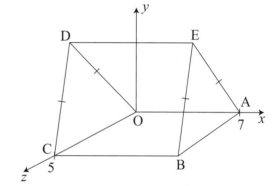

4 OPQRV is a rectangular-based pyramid. V is directly below the centre of the rectangular base. The pyramid has a height of 13 units. Write down the co-ordinates of O, P, Q, R, V.

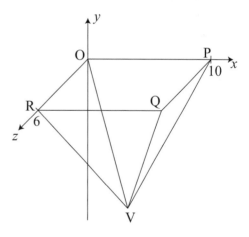

TASK E18.1

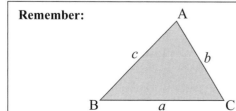

Remember:

$$\frac{a}{\sin A} = \frac{b}{\sin B} = \frac{c}{\sin C}$$

or

$$\frac{\sin A}{a} = \frac{\sin B}{b} = \frac{\sin C}{c}$$

Use a calculator and give all answers to 3 significant figures.

Find the value of each letter in Questions ① to ⑥

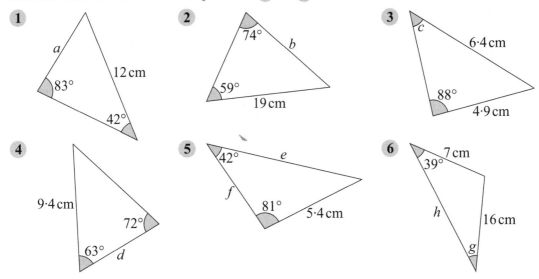

① *a*, 12 cm, 83°, 42°

② 74°, *b*, 59°, 19 cm

③ *c*, 6·4 cm, 88°, 4·9 cm

④ 9·4 cm, 72°, 63°, *d*

⑤ 42°, *e*, *f*, 81°, 5·4 cm

⑥ 7 cm, 39°, *h*, 16 cm, *g*

⑦ In triangle KLM, KM = 6·8 cm, ∠KLM = 78° and ∠MKL = 34°. Find the perimeter of triangle KLM.

⑧ Maddlestone is 28 km due north of Kenton. Howick is on a bearing of 137° from Maddlestone and Howick is on a bearing of 067° from Kenton. Find the shortest distance from Kenton to Howick.

TASK E18.2

Remember:

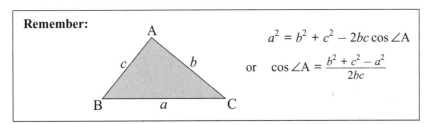

$$a^2 = b^2 + c^2 - 2bc \cos \angle A$$

or $\cos \angle A = \dfrac{b^2 + c^2 - a^2}{2bc}$

Use a calculator and give all answers to 3 significant figures.
Find the value of each letter in Questions ① to ③

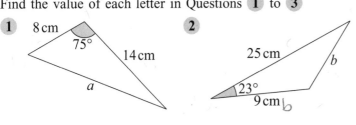

① 8 cm, 75°, 14 cm, *a*

② 25 cm, *b*, 23°, 9 cm

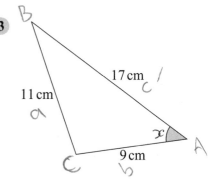

③ 17 cm, *x*, 11 cm, 9 cm

4 In triangle PQR, PQ = 32 cm, PR = 28 cm and QR = 21 cm.
Find the size of ∠QPR.

5 A boat sails due North for 41 km then travels on a bearing of 218° for 23 km.
The boat then sails back to its starting position. Find the total distance
travelled by the boat.

6 Alan is 14 km due east of Davina. Alan walks on a bearing of $x°$ and Davina
walks on a bearing of $y°$. They meet at a more southerly point when Alan has
walked 7 km and Davina has walked 10 km. Find x and y.

7 Find the perimeter of triangle ABC.

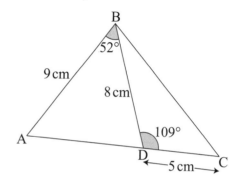

TASK E18.3

Remember:

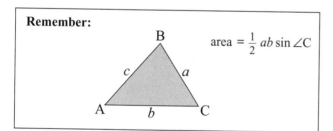

$$\text{area} = \frac{1}{2}\,ab\sin\angle C$$

Use a calculator and give all answers to 3 significant figures when appropriate.

Find the value of each letter in Questions **1** to **3**

1
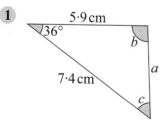

2
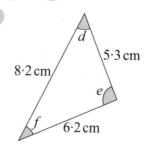

3
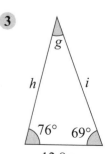

4 In triangle ABC, AB = 15·1 cm, BC = 29·7 cm and AC = 19·6 cm.
Find the area of triangle ABC.

5 Balloon A travels 15 km on a bearing of 029°.
Balloon B travels 39 km on a bearing of 043°.
  a How far apart are the balloons now?
  b On what bearing would balloon A have to travel
  in order to reach the position of balloon B?

6 If the area of triangle PRS is 127 cm²,
find the area of triangle PQR.

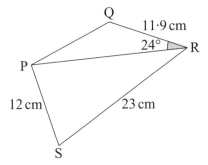

7 Hanif walks 6 km on a bearing of 159° then 9 km on a bearing of 252°. On what bearing
must Hanif walk to return to his starting point and how much further must he walk?

TASK E18.4

Use a calculator and give all answers to 3 significant figures when appropriate.

1 This pyramid has a square base
PQRS of side length 9 cm.
VM is vertical. M is the midpoint of PR.
Find
  a the length of PM
  b the height VM of the pyramid

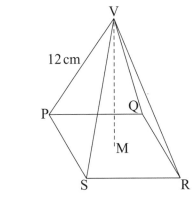

2 Find the following lengths in this cuboid.
  a QS
  b LS
  c KR

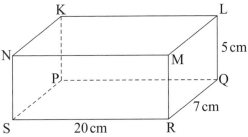

3 A man walks 30 m due West from the foot of an aerial mast which is 40 m
high. He then walks 50 m North. How far is he from the top of the mast?

4 This pyramid has a rectangular base ABCD which is horizontal. The vertex P is directly above the centre of the rectangular base. The perpendicular height of the pyramid is 27 cm. Find

   a AQ

   b AP

   c the area of the face PCD

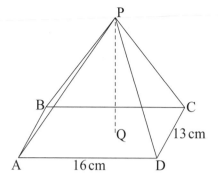

5 A cuboid is such that its height is 1 m longer than its width and its length is 2 m longer than its height. If the longest diagonal in the cuboid is 6 m then find the width of the cuboid.

TASK E18.5

Use a calculator and give all answers to 3 significant figures.

1 PQRSTUVW is a cuboid. Find

   a QV   **b** ∠QVU

   c WU   **d** ∠WUV

   e QW   **f** ∠QWU

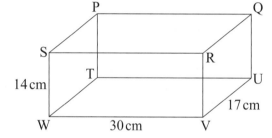

2 BC is perpendicular to CD. Find

   a AC

   b ∠BAC

   c CD

   d the angle between BD and the plane ACD

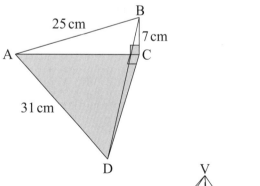

3 This pyramid has a rectangular base ABCD. VM is vertical. M is the midpoint of AC. Find

   a BM

   b VM

   c the angle between VB and the plane ABCD

   d ∠BVC

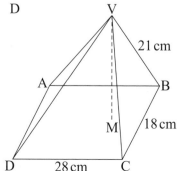

4 This diagram represents the roof of a house.

ABCD is horizontal with AB = 10 m and BC = 26 m. EF is horizontal. EF is 20 m long and 2 m above the horizontal plane ABCD.

AEB and DFC make the same angle with ABCD. BCFE and ADFE make the same angle with ABCD.

N is in the plane ABCD and is vertically below E. M is the midpoint of AB. X is the point on BC such that ∠NXC is a right angle.

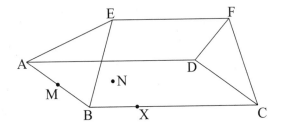

a Write down the lengths of EN and MN.
b Find the angle between EM and the plane ABCD.
c Calculate the length NC.
d Find the angle which the line EC makes with the plane ABCD.